Rebecca Probert is widely recognised as the leading authority on the history of marriage law and practice in England and Wales, a subject on which she has written extensively. Currently Professor of Law at the University of Warwick, she read law at St Anne's College, Oxford, took her LLM at University College, London, worked as a researcher at the Law Commission, and has lectured in family law since 1997. She has spent many years deeply engrossed in the large-scale genealogical case-studies which underpin the conclusions of her academic work. Her many TV and radio appearances include the BBC's *Who Do You Think You Are?*, *Heirhunters*, and *Harlots, Heroines & Housewives*.

Professor Probert is constantly adding to her body of research on the history of marriage and its application to genealogy, and would love to hear from family historians on any of the many topics raised in this book. Details of how to get in touch are on p. 203.

D1398943

Also by Rebecca Probert

The Changing Legal Regulation of Cohabitation: From Fornicators to Family, 1600 to 2011 (Cambridge University Press, 2012)

'This fascinating study takes to task the sloppy scholarship of earlier generations, which, on the basis of incomplete research, guesswork and a good deal of wishful thinking, drew unwarranted similarities between the ways people lived in the past and the way we live now.'

Professor Rosemary Auchmuty, *Journal of Legal History*

Marriage Law & Practice in the Long Eighteenth Century: A Reassessment (Cambridge University Press, 2009)

'The culmination of several years of painstaking archival work and detective work, this is a remarkable book that sets the record straight for scholars of marriage and sets new paradigms in our understanding of Georgian marriage habits and, incidentally, in standards of empirical research and exposition.'

Professor Joanne Bailey, *Journal of Legal History*

'This book will surely reinforce her standing as one of the foremost legal scholars of her generation.'

Professor Stephen Cretney, *International Journal of Law in Context*

Marriage Law for Genealogists (Takeaway, 2012)

'A must-have for every family historian'

Mocavo.com's '5 Essential Reference Books for British Genealogy'

'This book will greatly add to your understanding of marriage laws and help you in your research. It is a must for anyone seeking to understand the law or struggling to find a particular marriage'

Rootsweb.ancestry.com

DIVORCED, BIGAMIST, BEREAVED?

the family historian's guide to
marital breakdown, separation,
widowhood, and remarriage:
from 1600 to the 1970s

Rebecca Probert

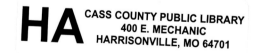

TAKEAWAY

First published in Great Britain in 2015
by Takeaway (Publishing)

1st edition, v. 1.0 LS

Takeaway (Publishing), 33 New Street, Kenilworth CV8 2EY

E-mail: rebecca.probert@warwick.ac.uk

British Library Cataloguing in Publication Data.
A catalogue record for this book is available from the British Library

ISBN 978-0-9931896-0-9

Foreword

Having written in depth about the legal and social aspects of how our ancestors married in *Marriage Law for Genealogists*, and having invited people to get in touch with any particularly puzzling marital relationships in their family trees, I was struck by the number who raised questions relating to the *ending* of marriages rather than to their formation—what precisely was the law on divorce, the prevalence of bigamy or long-term separation, or the truth about 'wife-sale'? Many correspondents had uncovered a bereaved husband apparently marrying his late wife's sister, while a surprising number had found an ancestor inexplicably marrying the *same* person twice (or even, on one occasion, *three* times!). Others questioned why an ostensibly eligible young widow might remain unmarried after losing her first and only husband.

As an academic historian of law, I had by then been investigating the landscape of marital breakdown, bereavement, and remarriage for some two decades already. As my body of research findings had grown, it had become clear to me that no single aspect could be neatly fenced off from the rest: a couple's decision to part ways—whether amicably or not, whether by consent alone, by written deed, or with a formal court order—cannot be understood without knowing how the law stood on divorce, conjugal rights, maintenance, and a host of other points. Desertion and bigamy cannot be understood without understanding the practicality of the legal options for ending a marriage, and appreciating how wider society viewed marital and pseudo-marital relationships; remarriage needs to be set within the context of social attitudes, average age at death, and other factors. These and many other issues did not easily fit within the scope of *Marriage Law for Genealogists*, and clearly deserved a book of their own.

So I am very grateful to all those who contacted me with queries and examples, including Andy Turner, Antony Marr, Bob Barber, Brian

Pollard, Sylvia Dibbs, Dick Mathews, Jill Kell, Julian Richardson, Patrick Cunningham, Penny Wythes, Percy Round, Roy Jones, Sam Riches, Steven Hollis, Stewart Armstrong, Anne Elder, Barry Smith, Raymond Pearson, Margaret Good, Cathy Soughton, Jacqui Simkins, Diane Towers, and Richard Brown. I have tried to anonymise cases sent to me by individuals, but as I have drawn extensively on reported examples of divorces and bigamies there is a chance that other readers will discover the antics of an ancestor in these pages!

I am also very grateful to Sam Hayday, who meticulously analysed the data from Cardington to ascertain the average duration of marriages within that cohort, and the circumstances in which couples remarried; to David Brookmann and Rachel Pimm-Smith, who have doggedly followed detected bigamists through successive censuses; to Melissa Maynard, who has been undertaking a project with me on the use of bigamy in divorce proceedings; and to my colleague Dr Maebh Harding, who guided me on the intricacies of overseas divorces. To all of them I owe not only much useful information but also many interesting conversations.

Table of contents

INTRODUCTION

In Charles Dickens' 1854 novel *Hard Times*, the millworker Stephen Blackpool seeks advice as to how he can free himself from his absent drunkard of a wife and marry his sweetheart Rachael. The answer is uncompromising: 'No how'. But Stephen persists, unable to believe that the law provides no remedy:

> *'If I flee from her, there's a law to punish me?'*
>
> *'Of course there is.'*
>
> *'If I marry t'other dear lass, there's a law to punish me?'*
>
> *'Of course there is.'*
>
> *'If I was to live wi' her an' not marry her—saying such a thing could be, which it never could or would, an' her so good—there's a law to punish me, in every innocent child belonging to me?'*
>
> *'Of course there is.'*
>
> *'Now, a' God's name,' said Stephen Blackpool, 'show me the law to help me!'*

Stephen's predicament neatly sets out the landscape of marital breakdown in England and Wales from the start of the 1600s right through to the twentieth century: his options, as he understood them, were to abandon his wife, or commit bigamy by marrying Rachael, or else live with her out of wedlock. Each choice had its implications—he could be pursued by the authorities for desertion, punished under the criminal law as a bigamist, or would bring shame upon Rachael and any children they might have together, who would be stigmatized by the law as illegitimate. He and his drunken wife might also have agreed to separate, but an informal agreement had no legal effect, and a formal separation order issued by a court was beyond the ken of a labouring man. Stephen also had, in theory, the option of divorcing his wife, but the procedure was out of the question for a man of his means and the grounds for divorce were restricted.

Even when, just a few years after *Hard Times* was written, the law was changed to make divorce easier and cheaper, Stephen would still not have been in a position to proceed, since it demanded that he travel to London, prove his wife had committed adultery, and find upwards of £40 to fund a petition. Then again, Stephen could wait until his wife died, but she might live for many years, stymying any possibility of happiness with Rachael.

Of course, for the entirety of the period under consideration—up to and including the present day—the majority of marriages *were* ended only by death. So dealing only with marital breakdown would give a very skewed view of our ancestors' lives, and *Divorced, Bigamist, Bereaved?* accordingly sets out to map all the various ways in which marriages might come to an end, and the circumstances in which individuals might embark on a second or subsequent marriage. Inevitably, though, there is more to be said in this context about the lives of those whose marriages broke down. The laws attempting to regulate such breakdown filled many tomes on lawyers' shelves, while the stories of those who experienced marital separation or breakdown are often far more fascinating and complex, and generated far more possibilities for us to follow up, than those of couples who were fortunate enough to enjoy just one long, happy marriage.

It is because of the richness of those stories that I have made use of illustrative case studies, and readers might find that particular stories resemble those in their own family tree. They are taken from a variety of contemporary sources, including reports of local sessions and assizes, magistrates' courts, church courts, divorce courts, and the Old Bailey. (Simply to keep footnotes to a minimum, I have not given exact dates for most of the newspaper articles cited. Readers who would like to follow up any such details are welcome to contact me for specific references.) I have also tried to link sources wherever possible, both to verify the details reported in the press or the court and to find out what happened after the legal case. This proved rewarding, not just in giving some indication of how divorce, bigamy, and bereavement were seen by the community, but also in revealing occasional overlaps between cases. As a result, some individuals with particularly colorful lives surface in different chapters as they experience separation, bigamy, divorce, remarriage to the same person, bereavement, and yet another remarriage!

Of course, in selecting illustrative stories it is important to set them in their broader context. It would have been very easy to fill these pages with some of the more outlandish tales of marital breakdown—sometimes tragic, sometimes entertaining, sometimes frankly bizarre. But we cannot evaluate these stories—or those of our own ancestors—without knowing what was typical of the time. So *Divorced, Bigamist, Bereaved?* also makes extensive use of statistical material to set lives in their broader context. Statistics from the mid-nineteenth century onwards are available from the Office for National Statistics and can be regarded as reasonably authoritative (although, given that they are derived from the information given on marriage registers, which was not always entirely truthful, they cannot be regarded as 100 per cent accurate). Figures from earlier periods are derived from smaller studies and should be taken as illustrative rather than definitive. Even so, particularly useful data about the likely duration of marriages can be derived from cohort studies of communities: having traced the marriages of thousands of couples as part of the research discussed in *Marriage Law for Genealogists*, I have now traced several hundred of these couples through their subsequent lives together until death parted them.

So the statistics and the stories need to be read together with the legal rules. All too often the facts of a single life will be too scant to make anything more than an educated guess about the experiences and motivations of the individual. But broader social histories can help us interpret our findings and ascertain how far an ancestor followed the life-course to be expected of a person born in their time, place, and station. By building up a body of individual examples, we can begin to see trends and patterns emerging, and by looking in more detail at the lives of those involved we can gain an insight into why they, and others, acted as they did.

There are of course dangers in attributing motives to past generations: one is that we think of them as sharing our own assumptions and beliefs; the other is that we see them as entirely different. Marital breakdown is such a commonplace of modern life that many people (including experts in the field) find it hard to accept that our ancestors did not resort to some kind of instant remedy if a marriage proved unhappy and divorce was unavailable; on the other hand, the greater likelihood of early death has led many to assume that people once had a different view of marriage altogether—more pragmatic, and less emotional. A further temptation is to merge the two ideas and assume that early death was itself a predictable substitute for divorce in past centuries. One popular genealogical guide suggests that:

> the lack of any means of legal divorce was nowhere near as big a problem in the nineteenth century and earlier as it would be today, for the rather grim reason that life expectancy was much shorter, and if you were dissatisfied with your spouse, you were unlikely to be shackled to them for thirty or forty years or more, since the chances of both of you living that long were not very high.[†]

Others have claimed that the duration of marriages has changed little over the centuries: in *The Second Book of General Ignorance*, the writers of the popular BBC TV series *QI* assert with apparent precision that:

> The average length of a British marriage is 11 years and six months, which is about the same as it was for 12th century peasants.

In actual fact, while the average duration of British marriages *that end in divorce* is indeed around 11½ years at present, the average duration of marriages *as a whole* is currently 32 years, a figure comparable to that in the nineteenth century.

While writing this present volume, it became clear that these and many other assumptions needed to be rethought. Accurately gauging the true extent of marital breakdown in earlier centuries might be an impossible task (especially before national censuses), but there is little to suggest that marriages broke down on anywhere near the same scale as today, and much to indicate that the vast majority of couples remained together until death claimed one or the other of them. And even if is true that nothing is certain in this life except death and taxes, few couples would have embarked on marriage expecting

† Annal and Collins, p. 128

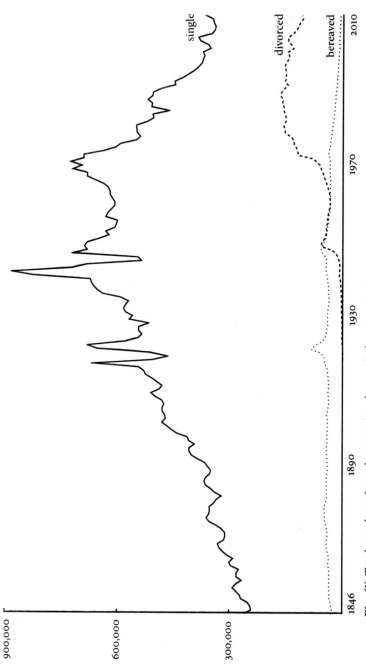

Fig. (i) *Total number of people marrying, by marital status, 1846–2010*

it to be cut short by a particularly early death, just as few couples today expect their marriage to be one of the minority that end in divorce. Nor was the Grim Reaper considerate enough to take only those spouses who were making the other's life a misery: there was no shortage of happy marriages cut short by early death, or of unhappy couples yoked together for thirty or forty years without redress.

Just as we need to be cautious in the motives we attribute to our forbears, so too we may need to think about the limits not only of our own knowledge but also of *theirs*. It is not uncommon, for example, to find an ancestor who (to judge from the details and handwriting on a marriage certificate) has clearly gone through a ceremony of marriage with a second spouse, yet fail to trace a death for the first. Even if there is clear evidence that the first spouse was living at the date of the second marriage, it might nevertheless be the case that the second marriage was valid—perhaps because the first had been *invalid*, or perhaps because of an intervening divorce—and that no crime had been committed. A divorce should, of course, be traceable; but a void marriage needed no decree of annulment, and the innocent explanation for an ancestor's second marriage—or, rather, their first *valid* marriage—may be lost to history. This did occur, for example, where somebody's first spouse was in fact already married, with cases of this kind surfacing quite regularly in the newspapers.

And even if a first marriage was perfectly valid, a second was not necessarily bigamous: in the case of a lengthy separation, either spouse might have genuinely believed that the other was dead, and remarried thinking they were free to do so. While today we may be able to work out from death records that an absent spouse was alive and well at the time of the second marriage, this might not have been known at the time. Whether someone in such a situation was liable to be charged with bigamy would also depend on the length of the separation and the reasonableness of the belief—factors that are not always easy to ascertain from the bare bones of census records, and almost impossible to determine when the only facts we have are the details of an ancestor's baptism, marriages, and burial.

Looking at all the different sources, we can say with a fair degree of certainty that remarriage after divorce accounted for only a handful of cases before the mid-nineteenth century, climbed from a few dozen to a few hundred each year from 1850 to 1900, rose to over a thousand in the wake of the Great War, and finally became the most common reason for a second marriage in the wake of World War Two (see Fig (i), p. 17). Remarriage after the death of a spouse, by contrast, accounted for many thousands of remarriages each year over the period covered by this book, although the proportion of widows and widowers who remarry has declined in line with increasing longevity. Bigamous marriages, of course, are the most difficult to quantify: throughout the nineteenth century there were around a hundred or so convictions every year, but this only tells us about the ones that were detected and prosecuted.

It is with divorce, however, that we will begin, since the difficulties in obtaining a divorce until relatively recently set in context the resort to other remedies, both legal and otherwise. We will then move on to look at why and how couples separated without obtaining a divorce, and examine the circumstances in which those who remarried might be guilty of bigamy. Bereavement and the remarriages of widows and widowers are considered next, while the final chapter looks at those intriguing cases where the same two people went through more than one a ceremony of marriage together. While some of these individuals never married anyone else, in other cases it transpired that there had been an intervening bigamy, divorce, or death, uniting all three themes of this book. I hope you find it as enjoyable to read as I did to research and write.

A NOTE ON PRE-DECIMAL CURRENCY

Since many of the case studies and quotations in this book refer to pre-decimal 'pounds, shillings, and pence' (or *l. s. d.*), some readers might find an explanation of terms useful.

One pound (£1, or 1*l.*) = 20 shillings (20/-, or 20*s.*) = 240 pennies
One shilling (1/-, or 1*s.*) = 12 pennies (12*d.*)
One guinea = 1 pound and 1 shilling
One sovereign = 1 pound (as a gold coin)
One crown = 5 shillings
One florin = 2 shillings

Two shillings and sixpence, then, would be written as 2/6*d.* or 2*s.* 6*d.*

A NOTE ON JURISDICTION

The book is limited to the law of England and Wales, which has been substantially one and the same since the sixteenth century and is generally known for reasons of brevity as 'English law'. The use of 'English' to mean both English and Welsh in this book is not intended in any way as a slight upon the beautiful nation of Wales, in which I have spent much time teaching and travelling, and which is, besides, the ultimate home of my surname. Scotland, by contrast, has always had its own distinct laws and is referred to only tangentially (regarding, for example, the status of marriages at Gretna Green). Ireland also has its own complex legal history which is beyond the scope of this book.

A BRIEF GLOSSARY OF TERMS

Certain terms recur frequently throughout this book, and it will be useful to set them out here for ease of reference and for clarity, and thematically rather than alphabetically, since their legal usage sometimes differs from their everyday meaning.

Adultery

It is important for genealogists to understand precisely what was being alleged when an ancestor was accused of adultery, but there is, I'm afraid, no delicate way of explaining! In English law, adultery is vaginal intercourse with somebody other than one's spouse: a married man cannot commit adultery with another man, nor a married woman with another woman, and even the most emotionally intense love affair is not adulterous if it does not involve sexual intercourse.

Bigamy

Bigamy is, essentially, the crime of going through a ceremony of marriage while already validly married to another person. It does *not* consist in being married to two or more persons at the same time, since the second and subsequent marriages are void in English law. Bigamy should be differentiated from *polygamy* (the state of being validly married to more than one person, which is possible in some jurisdictions outside England and Wales).

Decree absolute

The final decree of a court in proceedings for divorce, which ends an existing marriage.

Decree nisi

The provisional decree of a court in proceedings for divorce, which after a minimum period can be made absolute unless (Latin, *nisi*) sufficient cause is shown why this should not happen.

Petitioner (or petitioning spouse)

In divorce proceedings, this is the spouse who presents the divorce petition to the court asking for a decree ending his or her marriage.

Respondent

In divorce proceedings, the spouse upon whom the divorce petition is served.

Co-respondent

In divorce proceedings, a person with whom a respondent is alleged to have committed adultery.

Illegal

For the purposes of this book, an 'illegal' marriage ceremony is one which would expose one or both of the parties to a criminal prosecution. Though everyday usage often confuses 'illegal', 'void', and 'invalid', a marriage ceremony which is incapable of creating a valid marriage is only 'illegal' if it is in violation of a criminal statute (for example, in the case of bigamy).

Valid

A 'valid' marriage is recognised as a marriage by every court, and for all legal purposes. Any children born after the marriage are legitimate, and the marriage can only be ended by death or divorce.

Voidable

A 'voidable' marriage is one that may be annulled by a court but which is regarded as valid unless and until a decree of nullity is issued. It cannot be challenged after the death of either of the parties. However, before 1971 a decree of nullity operated retrospectively, so that the marriage was declared to have been void from the start, thus bastard-izing any children of the union.

Void

A void marriage is regarded by the law as never having existed. It is void from the start without any formal annulment by a court. However, while nothing that the parties later do can change a void marriage into a valid one, legislation may retrospectively validate marriages that would have been void at the time they were celebrated (see e.g. marriages within the prohibited degrees, p. 179).

There are a variety of ways to describe how a court may deal with a void or voidable marriage: it can 'avoid' it (i.e., make it void), inval-idate it, annul the marriage, declare it to be void, declare that it never existed, declare it to be invalid, or issue a decree of nullity. All of these are the same, and are equally correct.

~~~ **1** ~~~

DIVORCED

THE LAW AND PROCESS OF DIVORCE
REMARRIAGE AFTER DIVORCE

For most of the period covered by this book, divorce was so difficult to obtain that very few were granted, and the number of divorced persons who remarried was smaller still. Over the course of the twentieth century, though, the proportion of marriages that ended in divorce increased significantly. By the late 1940s the number of marriages involving one spouse who had been divorced was greater than the number of marriages involving a widow or widower.

But while it is not very likely that one of your ancestors succeeded in obtaining a divorce before the start of the twentieth century, and *highly* unlikely that they did so before the mid-nineteenth century, the law and practice of divorce forms an essential backdrop to understanding marital breakdown and remarriage more generally. Many of those who committed bigamy, for example, would not have done so had divorce been more readily available. Some of those who can be found living separate from their spouse in successive censuses might well have preferred to obtain a divorce to enable them to remarry had this option been open to them. A knowledge of the law relating to divorce and of the restrictions on obtaining a divorce at any given time is essential if we want to understand both bigamous remarriages and the failure to remarry after the *de facto* breakdown of a marriage.

This chapter will begin by setting out the law and process of divorce, in order to show what the experience of a divorced ancestor would have been. It then goes on to look at life after divorce. How likely was a divorced person to remarry? Whom could they legally marry,

23

and how could they go about it? And what did they actually do in practice?

For a period during the sixteenth century, it seemed likely that the law of divorce in England and Wales might change radically, since the Protestant Reformation was then being accompanied by intense debate across Europe as to whether the Catholic concept of the indissolubility of marriage should be retained. The matrimonial entanglements of Henry VIII led to cynicism among some that the law of nullity might be used strategically as an alternative to divorce, and in 1552, under Edward IV, proposals for divorce on the basis of adultery, cruelty, desertion, or 'mortal enmity' were considered. But Edward's early death and the succession of the Catholic Mary Tudor put an end to the chances of reform, and the issue was not revived under Queen Elizabeth. Alone within Protestant Europe, England and Wales maintained that marriage, once validly entered into, was indissoluble except by death. At the start of the seventeenth century, the courts emphatically reasserted that remarriage was not permissible even if the parties were formally separated by a decree issued by the church courts, and in 1603 legislation was passed making it a criminal offence to go through a ceremony of marriage while already married to another person (see p. 99). There matters rested until the 1660s.

From the 1660s to December 31st, 1857

From the 1660s, occasional exceptions to the idea that marriage was indissoluble began to be made, with private Acts of Parliament dissolving individual marriages. The first case was that of John Manners, Lord Roos, heir to the earldom of Rutland, whose marriage had broken down after less than a year, his wife Ann having blatantly committed adultery. For this the only remedy available was a decree from the church courts authorising them to live separately (a so-called 'divorce *a mensa et thoro*': see p. 75). John duly obtained this decree, but the fact remained that, so long as he remained married to the absent Ann, he would never be able to father a legitimate heir. For that, a valid remarriage was necessary, and so he petitioned Parliament to pass legislation permitting him to remarry. This unprecedented request led to considerable debate, but eventually, in 1670, an Act was passed declaring that it would be lawful for him to remarry during Ann's lifetime 'as if she were naturally dead.'

A precedent had been set, but there was no immediate rush to take advantage of this new possibility. The second parliamentary divorce was not granted until the 1690s, and during the first half of the eighteenth century there were a grand total of 14. While all were based on the adultery of the wife, the childlessness of the husband seems to have been an important motivating factor: until 1747, no divorce was granted to a man who had a living legitimate son, and petitioners played up the dynastic elements of their case.

By the second half of the eighteenth century, the numbers had increased to two or three per year, and the focus was shifting to the husband's right to rid himself of an erring wife and regain the 'comforts of matrimony' with a new spouse. The process for obtaining a private Act of Parliament became increasingly standardised and by the end of the century involved three distinct stages.

(i) First, the husband needed to sue his wife's lover for 'criminal conversation', an action that compensated him for what he had suffered. The monetary damages obtained from his wife's lover (which could range from as little as a farthing up to thousands of pounds, depending on what the jury considered the husband's losses were worth) could assist the husband in the subsequent stages of the divorce.

(ii) The husband was then expected to obtain a divorce *a mensa et thoro* from his wife in the church courts; this allowed them to live apart.

(iii) Only then could the husband petition Parliament to pass a private Act dissolving his marriage.

At every stage he would have to prove his wife's adultery afresh—to the jury, to the ecclesiastical judge, and to the Houses of Parliament. His own actions would also come under scrutiny: evidence that he had connived at or condoned his wife's adultery would reduce the damages awarded in the criminal conversation trial and would render it highly unlikely that he would succeed in the later stages.

RECORDS OF PARLIAMENTARY DIVORCES

If an ancestor did succeed in obtaining a private act dissolving their marriage, there is likely to be a wealth of surviving details about it. Each act will have been recorded on a vellum scroll and be available for consultation in the House of Lords library. The roll may well contain the original petition as well as other details of the process. More controversial cases may have been discussed in the newspapers, and from 1800 the more systematic reporting of parliamentary debates means that parliamentary discussions of the case may well have been recorded verbatim. You should also be able to find the terms of the Act itself in the statute book.

Key Fact: Before 1858, a divorce could only be granted by a private Act of Parliament.

The start of the nineteenth century saw the first woman succeed in obtaining a private Act of Parliament, admittedly under somewhat exceptional circumstances: Jane Addison's husband had run away with her sister Jessy, and, since Jessy's husband had already been granted a divorce from her, it would have been rather difficult to have refused Jane's petition. Exceptional cases do, however, make for limited precedents, and the view was taken that divorces would only be granted to wives in cases of 'incestuous' adultery of this kind. It was to be another 39 years before another wife managed in 1840 to persuade Parliament that a husband's bigamous adultery should also justify a divorce. With such narrow grounds, it is unsurprising that only two other women succeeded in obtaining private acts dissolving their marriages.

In sharp contrast to the four divorces granted to women between 1800 and 1857 there were 193 granted to men. Divorce, while still out of the reach of the majority, was no longer the preserve of aristocrats and the exceptionally wealthy. One scholar has gone so far as to suggest that 14% of those who procured a divorce could be considered to be working class, but given that the 42 men represented by this figure included 22 for whom no occupation was stated, and that the remainder included bankers, an attorney, and a farmer, this seems to be a rather expansive definition of working class.

Concerns began to be expressed about the amount of Parliamentary time that was being taken up by such private acts, while outside Parliament there were murmurings in bigamy cases that the rich could buy their freedom to remarry while the poor would suffer criminal sanctions if they did so. After a review by a Royal Commission and a number of abortive attempts at reform, legislation was finally passed in 1857 to create a new court with the power to grant divorces. The dissolution of a marriage and the right to remarry was no longer to be a matter of Parliament making individual exceptions to the general rule that marriage was indissoluble.

January 1st, 1858 through to the First World War

The new Court for Divorce and Matrimonial Causes took up residence in Westminster Hall at the start of 1858, taking over the court previously occupied by the Lord Chancellor. The improbably named Sir Cresswell Cresswell was appointed as the 'Judge Ordinary' who would be responsible for much of the day-to-day business of the court. The process for obtaining a divorce was intended to be a solemn and impressive one, with no fewer than three judges presiding over each case, potentially including the Lord Chancellor and the Lord Chief Justices, as well as other senior judges. It was not until Monday, May 10th, 1858 that the full court finally met to hear the first divorce cases, perhaps assuming that they would be relatively few in number. By May 26th, *The Times* was reporting that there were 173 petitions for divorce and judicial separation (see p. 80) waiting to be heard, far more than had been anticipated.

As we shall see, the new law was in many respects as restrictive as the old. Despite this, it can be seen as the most significant change to divorce law that this country has ever seen, both in terms of principle and in terms of its impact. Both its restrictions and its impact make it of interest to family historians: on the one hand, in explaining why an ancestor might have failed to obtain a divorce (or, more likely, had not even attempted to do so), and, on the other, in showing exactly what an ancestor must have gone through in their marital life in order to justify the ending of their marriage.

What had to be proved, and what would bar a divorce?

In many respects, the advent of judicial divorce in 1858 made little change to what justified the ending of a marriage. Adultery remained the only ground on which a divorce could be granted to a husband, and remained insufficient by itself to justify the grant of a divorce to a wife. Parliament had, however, expanded the range of additional factors that would, when combined with adultery, permit the granting of a divorce: if a wife could prove that her husband had 'aggravated' his adultery by incest, bigamy, cruelty, or two years' desertion, or that he had committed sodomy, rape, or bestiality, then she would be able to obtain a divorce.

If the spouse petitioning for divorce had *also* been guilty of adultery, however, or if he or she had connived at, condoned, or colluded in the respondent's adultery, then this would usually prevent a divorce being granted. In addition, cruelty, desertion, or neglect by the petitioning spouse might also lead the court to deny a decree, as would unreasonable delay in bringing the petition. In other words, success depended on the petitioner being able to prove one particular fact, but failure could result from a whole list of factors.

Key Fact: From 1858 to 1937, adultery was the only ground on which a husband could divorce his wife.

Key Fact: From 1858 to 1923, a wife could only divorce her husband on the ground of adultery plus an aggravating factor, or on the specific grounds of sodomy, rape, or bestiality.

Establishing adultery

Since adultery was regarded as a serious matrimonial offence, there had to be clear proof that it had in fact taken place. But given that it was rare for there to be witnesses to the act itself, circumstantial evidence would be accepted as sufficient:

> When Henrietta Farquharson petitioned for divorce from her husband Richard in 1860 she was able to give a lengthy list of his numerous infidelities during their short marriage. They had married in June 1859; he had been a Captain in the 24th Regiment

of Foot, while she was a rector's daughter from Derbyshire. At the time of their marriage he was already suffering from gonorrhea and infected her with the disease. Their only child was born prematurely and did not survive. During the last month of her pregnancy Richard was 'in the habit of frequenting the Turkish Divan in the Haymarket and the Portland Rooms in Foley Street and of meeting and associating with prostitutes there'; she was able to name three of them. In addition, Henrietta alleged that 'at divers times and places since the celebration of the said marriage and particularly at Portsmouth... and at Cork' he had committed adultery with 'divers women whose names are to your Petitioner unknown'. The judge, granting a decree of divorce in July 1861, commented that Richard's conduct had been such 'that it could only be characterized by terms which were hardly fit to be used in public.'

The court was not, however, always willing to take on trust the truth of allegations made, whether by the petitioner, the respondent, co-respondent or even witnesses. One wife was accused by her husband of having committed adultery with her groom, and another servant claimed to have seen them in the act; even then, the court thought it most unlikely that a wife would 'disgrace herself' in this way after twenty years of marriage—at least without taking precautions to conceal it from prying eyes!—and so dismissed the petition. The personal diary of another allegedly adulterous wife was dismissed as not being trustworthy, the supposed confessions being seen as the product of an overheated imagination. And in a third case the court refused to believe the testimony of a woman who claimed that the husband had seduced her when she was just twelve and had slept with her both before and after his marriage: the judge was reluctant to give credence to the 'unsupported testimony' of a woman of 'loose character' (the woman having also claimed that she had slept with two of the husband's brothers and another man). Her story, he thought, was 'not a probable one', since she had claimed to have sex with the husband on just two occasions since his marriage despite the fact that she was living just over the road from him—which raises questions about precisely how much sex one could have without being doubted as either unreliable or implausible!

If the petitioner had also committed adultery, then the Court for Divorce and Matrimonial Causes had a discretion whether or not to grant a divorce. There were essentially only three types of cases where a divorce *would* be granted to an adulterous petitioner:

(i) 'innocent' adultery, where the petitioner had remarried, believing the other spouse was dead or a divorce had been obtained;

(ii) 'unwilling' or 'forced' adultery, where the wife had been compelled by the husband to lead a life of prostitution;

(iii) 'condoned' adultery, where the petitioner's adultery had been condoned by the respondent and had not contributed to the respondent's adultery.

The Court firmly rejected the idea that greater leniency should be shown to adulterous petitioners. In one 1875 case where the husband had committed a single act of adultery—which his wife had forgiven—it was decided that he was not entitled to a divorce when she too later committed adultery; in fact, the Court suggested it was probable that his own conduct had 'tended to weaken her sense of the obligation of the marriage contract and so conduced to her guilt.'

Towards the end of the nineteenth century there were some signs of this highly restrictive approach being relaxed. In one 1895 case, the husband and wife had separated and signed a piece of paper agreeing each was at liberty to remarry. The husband duly did so, but on discovering that the agreement had no legal basis he returned to his wife. She then left him for another man and the husband petitioned for divorce. The judge granted it, deciding to overlook the husband's own adultery on the basis that he was 'a stupid man' in a humble rank of life who had genuinely thought his second marriage was valid.

Incest

If a wife could prove that her husband's adultery had been incestuous, then she would be able to obtain a divorce. 'Incestuous adultery' encompassed not only sex with blood relations but also with one's in-laws—i.e., with any person who would be within the prohibited degrees of marriage even if one's spouse had died. Despite this broader meaning—and the fact that marriage with a relative of a deceased wife, while forbidden by law, occurred on a sufficient scale to attract notice—this particular factor was only rarely invoked.

Rape, sodomy, and bestiality

All three of these provided independent grounds for a wife to divorce her husband: in other words, if a husband had engaged in sodomy with another man (or indeed an animal) it was not necessary to prove that he had also committed adultery with a woman. While all three were also criminal offences, it was possible for a wife to obtain a divorce even if the husband had not been convicted. In one case from 1898, the husband had only been convicted of a criminal assault, but his wife nonetheless succeeded in obtaining a divorce on the basis of his having raped the woman concerned.

This potential criminality did, however, mean that divorce judges might be cautious in accepting such allegations. As the judge declared in one case from 1862, in which sodomy had been alleged: 'the crime here imputed is so heinous and so contrary to experience, that it would be most unreasonable to find a verdict of guilty where there is simply oath against oath, without any further evidence, direct or circumstantial.'

Bigamy

A wife could also petition for divorce on the basis that her husband had aggravated his adultery by committing bigamy as well. On the face of it, this should have been a simple enough route to obtaining a divorce, particularly where the husband had already been convicted of bigamy. However, in the very first year of its operation, the new Divorce Court laid down certain rules and restrictions.

First, a wife had to prove to the Divorce Court that her husband had committed bigamy—the fact that he had already been convicted in a criminal court was not sufficient. On the other hand, if a wife wished to petition the Divorce Court it was not a legal *necessity* for her husband to have been convicted of bigamy. If anything, the criminal courts seem rather to have disapproved of spouses who were prosecuting simply as a preliminary to obtaining a divorce: in one case at the Old Bailey in 1872, the presiding judge, aware that criminal proceedings for bigamy had been taken 'with a view to a divorce', seemed to think that they were unnecessary and expressed his sorrow that the desire for a divorce 'should be considered a ground for [bringing] a criminal charge.'

This distinction between divorce proceedings and criminal prosecution was reflected in the fact that different definitions of bigamy applied in each case. The 1857 Act defined bigamy as simply 'the marriage of any person, being married, to any other person during the life of the former husband or wife.' Unlike in criminal proceedings, it was no defence to show that the parties had been separated from each other for seven years at the time of the second marriage and had heard nothing of each other during that time. So it was entirely possible for a person to be regarded as having committed bigamy for the purposes of obtaining a divorce but not to be liable for conviction in criminal proceedings.

Secondly, the phrase 'adultery coupled with bigamy' which appeared in the statute, was interpreted very narrowly. The bigamy and the adultery had to be committed with the same person; adultery with one and bigamy with another was not sufficient.

> In 1858 Janet Horn, née Prosser, sought to divorce her faithless husband Charles. Both had been on the stage, and the husband seems to have had a predilection for singers and dancers, since he had an affair with a singer and then went through a ceremony of marriage with a dancer, by whom he had three children. When he learned that his wife was taking legal proceedings he assumed that she intended to prosecute him for bigamy and left the country. The court was not convinced that there was sufficient evidence of adultery subsequent to the bigamous marriage, and granted the divorce on the alternative basis of adultery and desertion.

In addition, the fact that one's spouse had gone through a bigamous ceremony of marriage would not seen as sufficient evidence of their adultery! So unless there was specific proof of a sexual relationship, it would not be possible to obtain a divorce on this ground.

Cruelty

An adulterous husband's cruelty was relevant as a potential 'aggravating' factor entitling a wife to obtain a divorce, and in the first decade of the Divorce Court this was the factor most commonly cited by wives[†]. It was also a ground for the Court to grant a judicial separation (see p. 80). In addition, the cruelty of a petitioning spouse could also count *against* them if they were applying for a divorce, and could prevent the divorce being granted.

Before 1858, the church courts had required wives who wanted to obtain a decree of separation (a divorce *a mensa et thoro*, see p. 75) on the basis of a husband's cruelty to prove either actual injury or a reasonable fear that their husband would harm them physically. Initially, the Divorce Court adopted this same requirement. Its judges stressed that a judicial separation should only be sanctioned where there were 'grave and weighty' reasons to do so. In a case from 1861, it was held that a judicial separation should not be granted to a wife whose husband had taken her by the throat, shaken her, and thrown her down: the court's view was that only *repeated* acts of violence would justify the conclusion that she could not safely live with him.

Before long, however, judges began to move away from this insistence on violence. In one 1864 case, the husband's violence was not regarded as sufficiently serious to amount to cruelty, but his daily intoxication, adultery with servants, and tendency to bring prostitutes home *was* considered cruel, and the divorce was granted. If the adulterous husband contracted venereal disease as a result of his extramarital shenanigans, then knowingly communicating this to the wife would also constitute cruelty, as in the case of Henrietta and Richard Farquharson (pp. 28, 68, 70, 132, 145). Even *marital* sex might be held to amount to cruelty where the husband's sexual demands were seen as excessive, unnatural, or improper.[‡] By the end of the nineteenth century, the House of Lords had confirmed that non-violent conduct which resulted in injury to health would constitute legal cruelty.[1]

Desertion

If the husband had committed adultery and had deserted his wife for at least two years, the court would be able to grant her a divorce. In one case from 1862, the husband's desertion was easily established: he had gone to China and had failed to get in touch with his wife (he

† Hammerton, Table 4.2
‡ Savage (2009)
1 *Russell v Russell* [1897] AC 395

had, however, written to the woman with whom he had committed adultery, telling her that he had no affection for his spouse).

Key Fact: a wife could obtain a divorce on the basis that her husband had committed adultery and deserted her for at least two years.

Desertion did, however, require more than mere separation: in one case, a wife's divorce petition failed because she had gone to live with her sister after her husband had left home, and had made no enquiries as to where he was living. In another, the wife's refusal to return to her husband—17 years after their separation—meant that he could no longer be regarded as having deserted her. In short, any indication that the wife consented to the separation would mean that the complaint of desertion could not be made.

Key Fact: a wife could not rely upon her husband's desertion in a divorce petition if her behaviour had indicated consent to his desertion.

On the other hand, it was not necessary for the *husband* to be the one who left. The courts developed a concept of 'constructive desertion' to deal with the situation where one spouse had behaved in such a way that the other could no longer be expected to continue living in the same household. In other words, the spouse whose behaviour had forced the other to leave would be seen as having 'constructively deserted' them.

In one late nineteenth-century case, the wife had said that she was willing to stay with her husband if he would be faithful to her in the future. He refused, and the pair separated. When she subsequently petitioned for divorce, the court approved her decision to leave on the basis that this was the only course that 'a wife with any self-respect' could take in the circumstances. She was accordingly granted a divorce on the basis of his adultery and constructive desertion. Genealogists who have deduced from census data that it was the wife who had left the marital home prior to a divorce should bear in mind the possibility that she had been forced to leave by her husband's behaviour.

There were also ways of speeding up the process rather than waiting for the full two years to pass. In 1884, new legislation provided that a failure to comply with a decree of 'restitution of conjugal rights' amounted to desertion, and with immediate effect. How this worked in practice was as follows: after the adulterous husband had left the matrimonial home, the wife would write him an affectionate letter inviting him home. When he refused, she could petition the court for a decree of restitution of conjugal rights. When he still refused to comply with this order, she could petition for divorce on the basis of his adultery and desertion. Of course, whether or not this ruse proved successful depended on the husband either going along with it or having no inclination to return. If the affectionate letter inviting him home did indeed bring him back, the wife would have no legal remedy available to her.

Key Fact: after 1884, it was possible to establish desertion by showing the other spouse had failed to comply with a decree of restitution of conjugal rights.

Desertion by the petitioner, by contrast, might prevent the divorce being granted, at least if it occurred *before* the other spouse had committed adultery. While separation *after* the adultery would be regarded as a proper reaction to such errant behaviour, there was clearly a feeling that those who had been abandoned by their spouse were not entirely to blame if they formed a new relationship—or at any rate that the spouse who left should not be regarded as guiltless. In one 1882 case, for example, the man in question had been a most reluctant husband, only agreeing to the marriage when the woman became pregnant and insisting that she sign an agreement in advance that he would not be expected to live with her after the marriage. She not unreasonably decided to live with another man, but when her husband subsequently petitioned for divorce he was refused, on the basis that his desertion had been the cause of her adultery. As the judge noted, 'knowing her frailty, it was his duty, when he became her husband, not to have left her to the chances of falling, to which, abandoned as she was by him, she must have been exposed.'

Of course, the Court could sometimes decide that the spouse who had left the marital home had had good reason to do so:

> One of the early cases heard by the new court involved a young woman who had to explain why she had never actually lived with her husband. Ellen Du Terreaux's story was that she had married him aged just 16, without the knowledge of her family, while supposedly taking her morning walk in the Welsh seaside town of Aberystwyth. On returning to her family later that same morning, she apparently 'cried very much', and the truth came out. It was decided that the 36-year-old French teacher was not a suitable match for her, and she was packed off to the Continent. Her husband, not unreasonably, decided to remarry, and she then petitioned for divorce on the basis of his adultery and bigamy. The court granted the divorce, taking the view that it had been reasonable for her to separate from her husband on the basis that she must have been 'entrapped' into the marriage.

Connivance

A husband or wife who had apparently been indifferent to their spouse's adultery and done nothing to stop the affair would not be able to rely on that adultery at a later stage. So, for example, a husband who had witnessed the growing attraction between his wife and their lodger but did nothing to stop it was held to have connived at it. In another, even harsher, case, the fact that the wife was receiving a regular allowance as part of a separation agreement was seen as connivance in her husband's relationship with their former lodger.

Condonation

Taking an adulterous spouse back into the matrimonial home would generally be seen as amounting to 'condoning' the adultery, and this would prevent the innocent spouse from subsequently relying on the adultery to obtain a divorce. The rationale was that by not treating the adultery as a matrimonial offence of the highest order, a spouse essentially waived their right to rely on it in court. (Of course, this assumed that the innocent spouse had known the true facts; a wife who genuinely believed her husband's protestations of innocence and took him back was not prevented from subsequently seeking a divorce or judicial separation when she learned the truth.)

'Condonation' was not, however, the same as absolute forgiveness. The wronged spouse might well remain bitter and resentful, or refuse to treat the errant spouse with any affection, yet might nevertheless be held to have condoned the adultery: it was taking the other spouse back into the matrimonial home—and, crucially, the matrimonial bed—that counted. In one case, a wife agreed to break off her adulterous relationship and that same night made love to her husband. The following morning she said she had changed her mind, and the husband immediately left her. His subsequent petition for divorce was dismissed on the basis that he had condoned her adultery by having sex with her.

Misconduct on the part of an adulterous spouse could also 'revive' a former offence. So, for example, a wife who had taken back her adulterous husband might well change her mind if he subsequently treated her with cruelty, and the law allowed her to do so. In one case, the wife forgave the husband's cruelty and took him back, only to discover that he had also committed adultery. Since she had not known of his adultery, she was not held to have condoned it. In addition, the court held that his earlier cruelty was 'revived' by his wife's knowledge of his adultery, and the divorce was duly granted. As the court put it, 'all condonation was conditional' on subsequent good behaviour.

Collusion

The idea of 'divorce by mutual consent' had no place in English law at this time. Divorce was thought of as a remedy granted to an innocent spouse to free themselves of a guilty partner, and so any collusion between the pair would prevent the divorce being granted. The most obvious cases of collusion were where the husband and wife had agreed in advance that a bogus case would be presented to the court (for example, where neither was guilty of adultery but one agreed not to contest the allegation) or where crucial details were withheld from the court (for example where *both* had been guilty of adultery but one agreed to appear as the guilty party). Even an agreement as to the future arrangements for the children or assets might be seen as collusive and prevent the divorce being granted:

In 1893, John Steed Churchward petitioned for divorce from his wife Florence. The couple had married in 1887, when he was 44 and she only 19, but the union quickly proved unhappy. As Florence wrote:

'You are not surprised, I presume, at my leaving you. It had preyed on my mind for some time past, the fact that you did not want me; and that your opinion was that Poppie would be better looked after without me; and that everything I did was wrong. You have so often, over a mere trifle, told me "to go"; and I have now done so.'

She later admitted that she had not left home alone and advised John to proceed with a divorce. It was duly agreed that she would not defend the proceedings, and would even pay the costs and settle money on their daughter Poppie. Their agreement was openly disclosed to the court, but the Queen's Proctor argued that it amounted to collusion. The court agreed, and the petition was dismissed. Florence's affair seems to have been brief: by 1901 she was living in Portsmouth with relatives (the only evidence of her liaison being a six-year-old daughter), while her husband was lodging elsewhere. By 1911 both John and Florence described themselves as widowed. John died in 1930 aged 87, and Florence seven years later. The law had kept them married for 43 years—40 years after their relationship had begun to break down and 37 years after they had separated.

Q: *My great-grandmother divorced her husband in 1899, but I've been able to discover very little about how the marriage broke down. Can I assume anything about what she must have alleged in order to obtain a divorce at that time?*

A: To a degree, yes. Most likely, she would have been able to prove to the Divorce Court's satisfaction that her husband had committed adultery and had aggravated this by committing incest or bigamy, or by his cruelty to her, or by his deserting her for two years. It is also possible, though far less likely, that he had instead committed sodomy, rape, or bestiality. We can also infer that your great-grandmother had herself most probably not committed adultery, and that she had not condoned her husband's affair.

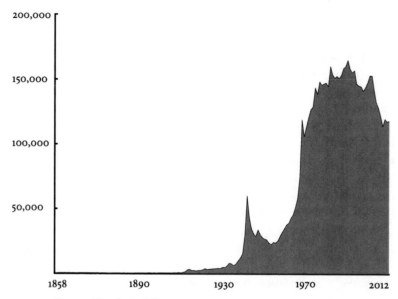

Fig. 1.1 *Number of divorces per year, 1858-2012*

What were the chances of successfully obtaining a divorce?

Despite the challenges posed by the restrictive grounds for divorce, and the expansive list of 'bars', the number of divorces granted under the new law was significantly higher than under the old system. In 1858, the first year of the new law's operation, there were 253 petitions—more than the Victorian legislature and judiciary had expected, but perhaps surprisingly low given the previous near-impossibility of obtaining a divorce. There were a handful of cases in which the courts were asked to grant a divorce on the basis of some long-ago act of adultery (see p. 67), but these were swiftly dealt with. The problem, of course, was that many of those who *would* have petitioned for divorce had it been available at the time had subsequently acted in a way that prevented them from doing so under the new act, whether by taking back their errant spouse or forming a new relationship of their own.

Throughout the nineteenth century and into the early years of the twentieth, the numbers continued to climb—not dramatically, but steadily. It has been estimated that even by 1911, more than half a century after the law had changed, only 0.2% of marriages were ending in divorce; to put it another way, in that year there were 6.5 million marriages in existence, and 902 petitions for divorce.† The success rate of petitioners, though, was relatively high. Perhaps surprisingly, the success rates of husbands were lower than those of wives. Sometimes this was on account of a failure to prove the alleged adultery, but more often it was due to their own behaviour. While the wife, of course, had to prove 'aggravated' adultery, this did not necessarily double her task: the aggravation might lie in the nature of the adultery (for example if it was committed with a relative—whether his or hers—or as the result of rape, or in the context of a bigamous marriage) or in its consequences (the cruelty of infecting the wife with venereal disease or his deserting her for the other woman).

Of course, those who had no case in law, or who were likely to have their petition dismissed, would be advised that they should not even make the attempt. Newspaper advice columns were full of responses to queries about when remarriage was possible. One replied to a husband (who simply signed himself 'Unfortunate') to advise him that 'unless you can prove your wife has committed adultery, you cannot obtain a divorce'. Another informed 'a Constant Reader' that 'no length of desertion dissolves a marriage'. It is clear that the number of divorces granted in this period certainly does not reflect the true demand, as the resort to other measures amply illustrates (see Chs. 2 and 3).

In addition, the likelihood of a legal bar to divorce being discovered was considerably increased by the appointment of an official known as the Queen's (or King's) Proctor in 1860. Since the court had rather more business than it had anticipated, arrangements were hurriedly put in place to deal with the demand and the three judges became just one. At the same time, processes were put in place to enable further investigation behind the scenes. Divorce became a two-stage affair: after hearing the evidence and being satisfied that there were grounds for divorce, the court would grant a 'decree *nisi*', but there would then follow a statutory waiting period before the 'decree absolute' was granted and the marriage finally brought to an end. The waiting period was initially to be three months, but in 1866 this was extended to six months. During that time, any person could intervene and

† McGregor pp. 37-38

FINDING PAPERS RELATING TO A DIVORCE

If an ancestor petitioned for divorce between 1858 and 1911, it should be possible to follow the legal proceedings, since the papers have been digitised and are available through commercial genealogy websites. However, much of the detail simply relates to the production of the evidence; for the court's assessment of the evidence it is necessary to see whether the case was one of the relatively few that was reported. The collected *English Reports* include some pre-1865 divorces; after 1865, a special set of reports was published for the Probate and Divorce courts. Both series are available in most university libraries. Newspapers tended to focus on particularly exciting stories or high-profile names, whereas the legal reports concentrated on those that resolved new points of law, so there is no guarantee that any given case was reported. Genealogists whose ancestors sought a divorce after November 1st, 1875, will note a change in the name of the court and personnel: the Court for Divorce and Matrimonial Causes became part of the new Probate, Divorce and Admiralty Division, with the Judge Ordinary as its President. The bringing together of cases relating to 'wills, wives and wrecks' (as one satirist put it) was something of an anomaly, but it remained so all the way through to 1970.

---

show that there was a reason why the divorce should not be made absolute—for example, that the petitioning spouse had committed adultery or that the spouses had colluded to obtain the divorce. In addition, the role of the Queen's Proctor was to investigate whether the divorce had been correctly granted: every undefended case would be examined, and action could also be taken in response to information supplied to his office. While intervention occurred in fewer than 10% of cases, it did often result in the decree being rescinded.

Who was most likely to obtain a divorce?

Social class

Gender, age, class, and location all affected the likelihood of an individual even trying to obtain a divorce. As we have seen, husbands were responsible for bringing the majority of petitions and accounted for around 60% of all divorces. While overall just as many women as men sought *some* form of matrimonial remedy, a significant minority of women petitioned for a judicial separation (p. 80) rather than a full divorce. This was the equivalent of the old divorce *a mensa et thoro* (p. 75), and did not permit either spouse to remarry. Its advantage was that it could be granted to a wife on the basis of either adultery *or* desertion *or* cruelty—rather than the more demanding combination of adultery *and* either cruelty or desertion or some other aggravating factor. Some wives who sought judicial separation might have done so because they did not have the necessary grounds for a divorce, but there is also some evidence to suggest that age could play a role: women who had been married for less than 20 years were more likely to seek a divorce than a separation. Those who had been married for longer than 20 years were slightly more likely to seek a separation, and those who had been married for more than 30 years were *much* more likely.[†] It would seem, then, that the desire to remarry (or at least the likelihood of remarriage after divorce) also influenced whether a woman was likely to seek a divorce. This should be borne in mind when looking at how long divorce petitioners had been married: figures for the close of the nineteenth century indicate that almost 15% of petitions were brought by people who had been married for five years or less, and a further 30% by people married between five and ten years. Only 12% of petitions were brought by people married for more than 20 years.[‡]

While there were plenty of examples of working-class petitioners (one of the first cases to be heard by the Court for Divorce and Matrimonial Causes involved a plumber and glazier from Bradford, described by *The Times* as being 'in humble circumstances'), the social profile of litigants remained definitely skewed towards the middle and

[†] Wright (2005), p. 279
[‡] McGregor, p. 49

upper classes. It has been calculated that in the first decade of judicial divorce, from 1858 to 1868, only 23% of litigants could be classified as 'working class'; 18% were lower middle class, and 31% were gentry, professionals, and prosperous businessmen.[†] Those members of the working class who did petition for divorce tended to be drawn from the ranks of artisans rather than unskilled labourers. And when set against the fact that the working classes accounted for around 80% of the population at this time,[‡] we can see just how unrepresentative the divorcing population was. In addition, there was a distinct geographical bias: London and the Home Counties provided more than half of all litigants in this period.[1]

To understand this situation—and the likelihood or not of an ancestor obtaining a divorce—we need to look at the cost of bringing proceedings for divorce.

Cost

As a result of the 1857 Act, the cost of a divorce had been reduced from hundreds to tens of pounds—at least where it was undefended. But to the court fees and the cost of legal advice had to be added the expense of travelling to London to attend court, and also the expenses of any witnesses who needed to travel. Sometimes, however, it was recognised that this was simply impracticable—for example where the adulterous relationship had taken place on the other side of the world—and the court would either allow the evidence of witnesses to be given on affidavit or appoint a Commission to take the evidence from the witnesses *in situ*. In other cases, though, unexpectedly lengthy hearings might suddenly increase the costs: as *The Times* pointed out in 1865, a husband who had struggled to save up the money for a divorce might be unable to afford to keep witnesses in London for several days, if the hearing looked like it was going on that long.

So there was a degree of uncertainty for potential petitioners as to how much a divorce might cost. Advice columns in newspapers were reluctant to be drawn into giving any specific figures. It was, as

[†] Savage (2011)
[‡] Rowntree and Carrier
[1] Savage (1992)

was regularly pointed out, impossible to say without knowing all of the circumstances of the case - including the income of the inquirer, since solicitors might well accept less than their due when acting for poor clients. Publications such as *Reynolds's Newspaper* and *Lloyd's Weekly Newspaper*, which had a largely working-class readership, do not give the impression that divorce was out of the reach of their readers on financial grounds. Advising on when it was possible to remarry without risking prosecution for bigamy, it was suggested that it would be better to apply for a divorce 'which, under the circumstances you mention, you could readily obtain at a moderate cost if you employ an experienced attorney.' The absolute minimum, however, was thought to be about £40. This tallies with the estimate given to the Royal Commission in the first decade of the twentieth century that an undefended divorce would cost around £40-£45, if the petitioner lived near London and no witnesses had to be called, but that more complicated cases could still cost up to £500. There are certainly examples in the case-law where the costs exceeded that sum.

> **Key Fact:** The cost of divorce varied widely, starting at something in the order of £40 but potentially reaching upwards of ten times that sum, depending on whether or not it was contested.

So how were these costs actually met, and how far might the potential costs deter individuals from even seeking a divorce in the first place?

One might expect the high cost of divorce to be more of an obstacle to women than to men: after all, at the time the 1857 Act was passed, a woman's property belonged to her husband upon marriage and this was not to change for some years. Yet the very fact that a woman's property became her husband's upon marriage meant that her husband had a duty in return to maintain her. As a result, *he* was responsible for the costs of the case where she could not afford them. So the court might, for example, require a husband to pay a sum of money into court or to give security to meet his wife's costs of trial, and could send him to prison if he refused to pay.

The court did however recognise that there were many husbands who were simply unable to find the resources to fund a divorce: in the 1859 case of a wife seeking to divorce her bricklayer husband who only earned a little over a pound per week, it was held that the man would not be punished if he could not pay. But since a wife at this time had limited contractual capacity, she could not be held liable either. In such cases, where neither could be held liable, it was the wife's legal advisor whose work did not receive recompense. The unfortunate result was that, as the Women's Co-operative Guild later noted:

> Solicitors will not take up a case where the husband depends on weekly wages. The prospect of payment is too uncertain. The liability of the husband is clearly meant to benefit lawyers, not women. Where there is money they are certain of their fees. Where there is none, the public get no justice.

Where it was the husband who was petitioning for divorce, there was one other person who might be required to pay the costs of the suit: the court would consider whether the man with whom the wife had committed adultery should shoulder the blame—and the costs. If the husband had previously tolerated his wife's conduct, or if the parties were already separated, the co-respondent was seen as less blame-worthy. But a man who 'invaded the house of the husband' would be condemned in costs, and might also be required to pay damages to the aggrieved husband. There was, however, no equivalent procedure for women to pay damages to the wives whose husbands they had inveigled away!

One final option was what was known as the *in forma pauperis* procedure. This was a form of assistance offered to the very poorest—those who could prove that they were earning less than 30s. a week and had less than £25 to their name (though this sum was later to change: see below, p. 47). Large swathes of the working classes would have been eligible: even on the eve of the First World War, the average weekly wage for unskilled labourers was only around 22s. But the number of applications remained low, no doubt in large part because the financial assistance provided did not cover *all* of the costs of obtaining a divorce: while successful applicants would be relieved from the obligation to pay court fees (around £6), they still had to pay other expenses, and it has been estimated that the average sum required from even a 'pauper' petitioner would have been between £12 and £21.[†] Finally, applicants had to find a solicitor and barrister willing to handle the case free of charge. Although there were lawyers who volunteered their services, they may have been understandably reluctant to take on more complex cases. As one newspaper somewhat discouragingly advised an inquirer: 'as this would be a troublesome case we doubt whether you would find [a solicitor] willing to act for you if you sued *in forma pauperis*.' It is small wonder that there were only about 15 cases brought under this procedure each year.

Overall, then, while the 1857 Divorce and Matrimonial Causes Act had made divorce considerably cheaper to obtain, there were still some who simply could not afford it. Some began proceedings but ran out of funds:

> *Charles Hanff, who was convicted of bigamy in 1891, had at least tried to end his first marriage by legal means. Having had a varied career as acrobat, piano-player, and photographer, he separated from his first wife in 1888 and apparently spent £40 on his petition for divorce before running out of money to see it through. Had he confessed as much to his second wife he might have been treated more leniently: as it was, his claim that he believed his first wife had died was rather undermined by the evidence that he had said that he would 'have to risk it' when telling a friend of his planned second marriage.*

One of the wives who responded to the *Daily Telegraph* debate entitled 'Is marriage a failure?' in the 1880s described the restrictions in passionate terms. Signing herself 'A Working Woman', she explained that she had discovered her husband to be a drunkard:

> 'A broken-hearted, forsaken wife, I resolved to leave him. We have lived apart now for the last ten years... I know he is living in adultery with another woman, but a divorce I cannot get because I have not the means. I am like a bird beating her wings against the bars of the cage, and there is no escape.'

---

† Gibson, p. 68

From the First World War through to December 31st, 1937

While the outbreak of war in 1914 brought no change to the law on divorce *per se*, it did mark the point at which the number of divorces began to move sharply upwards. By 1918, divorces had exceeded 1,000 for the first time ever, and by 1920 they exceeded 3,000. The backlog created by the unprecedented number of divorce petitions led in turn to an important change in the process of obtaining a divorce. An Act passed in 1920 made it possible for undefended divorce cases (together with those brought under the Poor Persons' Procedure, as the *in forma pauperis* procedure had been renamed in 1914) to be heard at the local assizes rather than exclusively in London. This came into operation on October 12th, 1922, and as well as enabling cases to be dealt with more quickly had the additional advantage of lowering the costs for provincial petitioners. Petitions could be filed in one of the 26 District Registries, and the case would then be heard at the nearest assizes.[†]

Key Fact: From October 12th, 1922, it was possible for the first time to obtain a divorce at a court sitting outside London.

Even so, the bulk of cases continued to be heard in London, and even provincial petitioners might have to travel some way, since not all assizes had the power to deal with divorce cases.

Alongside this change, there were a number of others directly aimed at making divorce more affordable. One was the raising of the limits under the Poor Persons' Procedure: from 1914, litigants with capital of up to £50 (and in exceptional cases £100) would be eligible for assistance, although in 1920 the requirement that they should also be earning less than £2 (or exceptionally £4) per week was added. As a result, between 1914 and 1937 a significant minority of petitioners (20-40%) benefited from financial assistance. Even so, the existence of a far wider demand for divorce can be seen from the fact that only a minority of applicants for financial assistance actually went on to file for divorce: out-of-court expenses still had to be paid, and many could not afford this. It was estimated that even an undefended divorce case would cost around £50.[‡]

[†] Gibson, p. 87
[‡] Gibson, p. 88

The social upheaval wrought by the First World War also facilitated changes to the grounds for divorce. Proposals to give husbands and wives (almost) equal rights in petitioning for divorce had been mooted before the war, but it was the demands of the war that fostered a climate receptive to change. In addition to women's important role in war-work and the post-war progress towards equal citizenship, a post-war surge in the numbers of petitions for restitution of conjugal rights heightened public awareness of the way in which such petitions were used strategically in order to obtain a divorce. Even so, it was only after considerable discussion that legislation was passed in 1923 finally relieving wives of the necessity of proving 'aggravated' adultery in order to obtain a divorce. The percentage of petitions filed by wives immediately increased to around 60%, and remained consistently above 50% during the 1920s and 1930s.

Key Fact: From July 18th, 1923, a wife could obtain a divorce simply on the basis that her husband had committed adultery, without having to prove any additional 'aggravating' factors.

The first case to be heard under the new Act was that of Bittleston v Bittleston, *in November 1923. The couple had married in 1907, but between 1914 and 1919 the husband had been on active service. His infidelity had led to a separation, and a subsequent reconciliation proved unsuccessful. Mrs Bittleston had began proceedings for restitution of conjugal rights on the basis that Major Bittleston had left her for another woman, but when the new law came into force she abandoned this suit (indicating that restitution was not her aim) and instead filed for divorce. As the President of the court noted, the case illustrated 'what has been common knowledge in this Court, that where there had been adultery it was almost an inevitable consequence that the guilty party deserted the innocent party.' The new Act, he noted, simply relieved the wife of having to bring two sets of proceedings.*

The 1923 Act did not, however, equalise the grounds for divorce entirely. Sodomy, rape, and bestiality all remained independent grounds for divorce for wives, but a husband whose wife engaged in a lesbian affair would be unable to obtain a divorce as this did not constitute adultery. Given that very few petitions had ever been based on this group of grounds, though, it was hardly a major advantage! In addition, while a wife no longer *had* to prove 'aggravating' factors, a surprising number of petitions continued to be granted on the basis of adultery plus desertion (or, more rarely, cruelty or bigamy), throughout the 1920s. By the close of the decade, however, they were a dwindling number.

A second significant change to divorce law occurred in the courts rather than in Parliament. The fact that the petitioner had also committed adultery continued to be a reason for the court to refuse to grant a divorce, but judges began to exercise their discretion more broadly. Whereas previously they had looked back at the circumstances under which the adultery had been committed, from the 1920s they began to focus on the potential for a couple in an adulterous relationship to marry. This shift was instigated by a case involving a soldier who returned from the war to find that his wife had committed adultery; he in turn then began a relationship with the family friend to whose care he had entrusted his children. It was felt to be in the interests of all concerned that she and the soldier be able to marry, even though he had already committed adultery with her. During the 1920s it became a regular occurrence for the court's discretion to be exercised in this way and more requests for this to be done were also made: the exercise of the court's discretion had been sought in a mere 45 cases between 1857 and 1909, but in a staggering 690 between 1920 and 1929. Discretion would not, however, usually be exercised in favour of those whom the court regarded as 'promiscuous', or who had attempted to conceal adulterous relationships from the court.

> **Key Fact: During the 1920s and early 1930s, judges became increasingly willing to grant divorces despite the adultery of the petitioning spouse, if this would enable the petitioner's new union to be 'regularised' by marriage.**

Divorce was beginning to become routine. According to one barrister, by the 1930s the hearing of undefended cases (which constituted the vast majority of all cases) was brisk:

I understand that an undefended divorce now takes five minutes, or less than 10 minutes. This is what takes place; There is no speech by counsel. He merely gets up—I assume it is a wife's petition—and he says: 'Your Lordships, this is a wife's petition. Mrs.—whatever her name is—will you go into the box?' He then asks her about 12 or 15 questions, and asks her to identify a photograph. She then walks out of the box, and ready to walk into the box is the agent who served the papers on the husband. He goes in and identifies the photograph, and says he found the husband living with another woman. 'That is my case, my lord,' says counsel; 'I ask for a decree.' The judge nods his head and says: 'So be it,' and it is finished. There is a queue all nicely arranged by the usher so that no time is wasted.[†]

It has been noted as 'one of the ironies of history' that perhaps the best-known of all twentieth-century divorces—that of Mrs Wallis Simpson—was swift and businesslike, taking place in the Assize Court at Ipswich before a judge who did not specialise in matrimonial law.[‡]

January 1st, 1938 through to December 31st, 1970

By the 1930s, further reform was being discussed. There was much mockery of what had come to be known as 'hotel divorces': cases in which the husband and wife had agreed to part, with the husband nobly pretending to be the guilty party and supplying 'proof' of his adultery by the simple expedient of booking into a hotel and being found in bed with a woman by the chambermaid. Evelyn Waugh satirised the process in his 1934 novel *A Handful of Dust*: the wife of a man 'of very rigid morality' pretended to be 'the other woman' so that they could be caught red-handed in a fictitious adultery. Of course, the husband might well be the guilty party, but still a hotel made a useful location to supply the evidence of adultery by disinterested witnesses. Major Bittleston, whose wife was the first to obtain a divorce under the 1923 Act (above, p. 48), had apparently already spent time away with another woman, but the evidence of his adultery was supplied by a short stay at the Piccadilly Hotel.

[†] *Hansard* 8/11/1937: col 1449
[‡] Cretney, p. 280

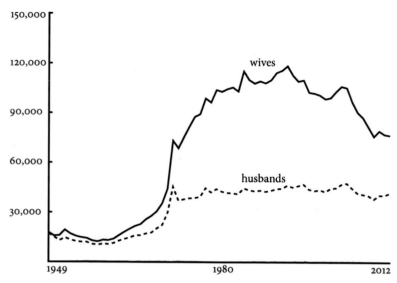

Fig. 1.2 *Divorces granted to husbands and wives, 1949-2012*

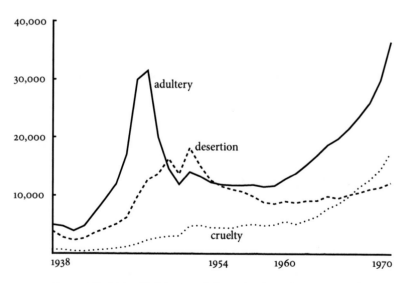

Fig. 1.3 *Petitions filed (1938-70), by grounds cited.* Note the massive spike in adultery petitions after World War Two. Petitions for insanity, presumed death, rape, sodomy, and bestiality are too few to show at this scale.

Such mockery of the law had its effects. A.P. Herbert, whose satirical novel *Holy Deadlock* had depicted the difficulties of a young couple who had fallen out of love but were unable to obtain a divorce, was elected to Parliament and campaigned for change. The ensuing Matrimonial Causes Act of 1937 allowed either a husband or wife to obtain a divorce on the grounds of cruelty, desertion for three years, or incurable insanity, in addition to the existing ground of adultery.

The Matrimonial Causes Act came into effect on January 1st, 1938, and the result was a sharp increase in the number of divorces. In 1937 the total had stood at a little under 5,000; the following year it jumped to over 7,500, and in 1939 to over 8,000. That this was due to the new grounds available can be seen from the fact that petitions based on adultery actually fell; by contrast, over a third of all divorces in 1939 were granted on the new ground of desertion for three years, and a further 10% on the basis of either cruelty or incurable insanity. Husbands and wives were equally likely to allege desertion, but wives were far more likely than husbands to seek a divorce on the basis of cruelty.

At the same time, the possibility of obtaining a divorce within a very short period of the wedding was curtailed: from the start of 1938, no petition for divorce could be filed within the first three years of a marriage, unless a petitioner could show either that they would suffer 'exceptional hardship' or that the other spouse was guilty of 'exceptional depravity'. This had been included in the 1937 Act as something of a concession to those concerned that any widening of the grounds for divorce might undermine marriage. The justification for this waiting period was to prevent newly-weds from rushing into a divorce, although there was no requirement that the couple should remain together during that time or that they should be encouraged to take active steps to save their marriage. It was also intended that there should be no slackening of the responsibility on the courts to inquire whether there had been collusion, connivance, or condonation and to dismiss the petition if there had been.

Within a couple of years, though, the impact of the 1937 Act was swallowed up in the far greater impact of the Second World War. After initial falls during the early years of the war, the number of divorces climbed to over 15,000 in 1945, and then to over 60,000 in 1947, an increase of more than ten-fold during a single decade. Adultery accounted for 71% of all petitions in 1946 (Fig. 1.3), and a higher proportion (63%) of petitions were brought by husbands than by wives, reflecting the fact that a wife's wartime adultery was generally easier to prove than that of a husband.[†]

Attempts to deal with this increase led in turn to divorces becoming more accessible: from January 1st, 1947, it was possible for a divorce to be granted by a 'Special Commissioner of Assize' at one of a large number of designated 'divorce towns', as well as by a judge presiding over the local assizes. These new 'Commissioners' were, in fact, county court judges wearing different robes, but the special title was intended to convey the impression that divorce remained a dignified matter.

Key fact: after January 1st, 1947, most divorces were heard outside London.

A more minor change that took place in 1946 was the shortening of the period between decree *nisi* and decree absolute from six months to six weeks, meaning that remarriage could take place sooner.

Q: *My paternal grandparents split up in 1947 and divorced in 1952. Would I be able to find the documentation that would tell me why their marriage failed?*

A: Desertion and adultery were the most commonly cited grounds, accounting for around 90% of divorces in 1952. Given the lapse of time between separation and divorce, desertion may well have been the ground relied on in this case. However, it may not be possible to confirm this. Unless the case involved a novel point of law, particularly scandalous facts or a well-known couple it is unlikely to appear in newspapers or law reports. Nor is it likely that there will be any surviving court documentation: while copious case files were kept in earlier periods, this is not the case after 1937, largely due to the increase in the number of divorces around this time. Nonetheless, you should be able to find out where the divorce was granted by requesting a search

[†] McGregor p. 41

for the decree absolute from HM Courts & Tribunal Services. This will tell you whether the case was heard in London, or in one of the newly designated 'divorce towns'. Around two-thirds of divorces were heard outside London in 1952, with all but a fraction being undefended.

Legal aid

Further change was to occur as part of the package of welfare reforms promoted by the Attlee Government in the wake of the war. The passage of the Legal Aid and Advice Act 1949 provided more generous financial assistance for those on lower incomes. The Act came into force on October 2nd, 1950, and in the first year of its operation almost two-thirds of those petitioning for divorce were legally aided. Wives in particular benefited from this new scheme, with over 70% of female petitioners for divorce in 1951 having financial assistance. All these changes had their impact on the divorcing population: by the 1950s, the profile of petitioners was, in occupational terms, roughly comparable to that of the population as a whole.[†]

Key fact: after the introduction of legal aid in 1950, cost ceased to be an obstacle to obtaining a divorce.

Interviews with working-class women about this period indicate that while there had always been some marriages that broke down, this had been much rarer before the war and more likely to result in separation rather than divorce; after the war, however, 'divorce was increasingly likely to be the outcome'.[‡] As one social scientist commented in the 1950s, when noting that wives once again accounted for the majority of petitions, the figure was likely to have been 'inflated by a number which would have been pursued earlier if the petitioners had not been too poor to obtain access to the divorce court'.[1]

---

† Rowntree and Carrier
‡ Roberts, pp. 107-8
1 McGregor, p. 41

The shift to irretrievable breakdown

Despite a number of attempts at reform during the 1950s, the grounds for divorce remained those established in 1937; but change did occur as judges interpreted the existing grounds more generously. Despite repeated assertions by judges and politicians that divorce should not be allowed simply because a couple did not want to be together any more, the concept of 'cruelty' came to encompass an increasingly wide range of behaviour, and to be relied on in an increasing proportion of cases. Desertion, meanwhile, was interpreted in a way that made sense in the context of both increased home-ownership and post-war housing shortages. It was recognised that those whose marriages had broken down might have nowhere else to go, and in 1949 the Court of Appeal held that desertion could be established where the parties were living separate lives under the same roof.

In addition, during this period a divorce could still be denied on the basis of a whole range of factors. While the courts were increasingly likely to exercise their discretion to grant a divorce even if the petitioner had also been guilty of adultery, they were still reluctant to do so if there was no possibility of the divorce leading to a new marriage. In 1947, a man who was cohabiting with his brother's former wife was denied a divorce, since as the law then stood a marriage between them would have been within the prohibited degrees (see p. 179). In addition, collusion remained an absolute bar to a divorce until 1963.

During this period it was also widely recognised that there were many who simply could not obtain a divorce. Interestingly, the focus of concern had shifted from the innocent spouse to the *adulterous* spouse: increasingly, people who were unable to obtain a divorce were nevertheless forming new relationships and families, but they were simply doing this outside marriage. The villain of the story had become the spouse who chose *not* to invoke the other's adultery as grounds for a divorce; the new hero and heroine, by contrast, were those living (as one MP was to put it) in 'stable alliances' that were marriages in all but name and which the vast majority would wish to formalise as soon as possible.

In 1966 a new law reform body, the Law Commission, claimed that 'around 40 per cent' of illegitimate children were 'born to couples living stably together but debarred from marrying by the still-existing marriage of one or other partner.' It claimed that, if divorce were to be made more widely available, 'about 180,000 living illegitimate children could be legitimated' by the remarriage of their parents. The accuracy of these figures might be debatable, but their impact was undeniable: legislation was passed in 1969 making 'irretrievable breakdown of marriage' the sole ground for divorce. Such breakdown still had to be proved by one of five facts whether adultery, unrea-

	what a husband needed to prove	what a wife needed to prove
January 1st, 1858 to July 17th, 1923	adultery	any *one* of: incestuous adultery; adultery with *either* bigamy *or* cruelty *or* desertion; rape; sodomy; bestiality
July 18th, 1923 to December 31st, 1937	adultery	any *one* of: adultery; rape; sodomy; bestiality
January 1st, 1938 to December 31st, 1970	any one of: adultery; cruelty; desertion for three years; incurable insanity	any one of: adultery; cruelty; desertion for three years; incurable insanity; rape; sodomy; bestiality
Since January 1st, 1971	'irretrievable breakdown of marriage', as evidenced by any one of: adultery; unreasonable behaviour; desertion for two years; separation for two years (with the other party's consent to the divorce); separation for five years	

Table 1.1 *The changing grounds for divorce, from 1858 to the present day*

sonable behaviour, desertion for two years, or separation for either two years (if the spouse consented) or five years (if the spouse did not consent). The similarity of the first three with the old fault-based grounds should not obscure the two major innovations that were made: the possibility of divorce by consent, and the possibility of divorcing a spouse guiltless of any matrimonial offence against his or her consent.

January 1st, 1971, through to the present day

The new legislation came into force on January 1st, 1971, and remains the current law of divorce. At this point we move into the realm of the modern family lawyer rather than the family historian. It is, however, worth noting the immediate impact of the new legislation in order for genealogists to be able to gauge the extent to which divorce had not previously been an option for their ancestors. There was, as was only to be expected, a dramatic jump in the number of divorces, from 50,581 in 1969 to 119,025 in 1972. But the new ground of five years' separation accounted for over 20% of these, and the fact that a significant proportion of petitioners were over the age of 60 strongly suggested that it was being used to clear a backlog of marriages that had been broken for some time. Divorce had finally become available as a legal solution in all cases of marital breakdown (see Fig. 1.1).

> **Key Fact: Since January 1st, 1971, 'irretrievable breakdown' has been the sole ground for divorce, although it can only be proved by evidence of one of five facts.**

So, it was only in the 1970s that an unhappy spouse could be certain of obtaining a divorce sooner or later, and divorce rates might well have been higher in earlier decades and centuries had greater facilities for divorce been available. The choices and actions of our ancestors have to be seen against that background.

REMARRIAGE AFTER DIVORCE

In many respects, the history of divorce is all about the right to remarry. After all, all of the other incidents of marriage could be dealt with by other means: an ecclesiastical court could order that the husband and wife were entitled to live separately; the pair could enter into a contract setting out how any property was to be dealt with; and each could make a will excluding the other from any provision in the event of their death. The one thing they couldn't achieve by private agreement was the right to enter into a second, legal marriage during their joint lifetimes. This aspect of divorce is particularly clear in the early petitions to Parliament: the men seeking a private Act of Parliament in the late seventeenth and early eighteenth centuries did so largely because they wanted to be able to ensure they had a legitimate heir to inherit their estates, while those doing so in the later part of the eighteenth century emphasised how they had lost the comforts of matrimony on account of their spouse's adultery. The desirability of remarriage was also, as we have seen, a major theme in the divorce reforms of the late 1960s, whereby the 'stable illicit unions' resulting from the restrictive grounds for divorce were to be converted into successful second marriages.

But what was the likelihood of remarriage after divorce in past centuries and decades? Were there any legal rules affecting who or how one could remarry? And *who* precisely remarried? Did a divorcee's likelihood of remarrying depend on whether they were male or female, the guilty party or the innocent spouse? Answering these questions is no easy matter, but the sections that follow draw on my most recent research to shed light on them.

Did divorcees remarry?

Even the very basic question of precisely what proportion of divorces was followed by a remarriage is difficult to answer. While the official statistics on marriage did begin to provide data on the remarriages of the divorced from the late 1850s, these calculations were based on those who described themselves as divorced in the marriage certificate, and not everyone chose to do so:

> *The very first case to be heard before the new Divorce Court*
> *on May 10th, 1858, was that of Norris v Norris and Gyles. A*
> *divorce was duly granted, and the now ex-Mrs Norris married the*
> *co-respondent, the Reverend Gyles, just three months later. In this*
> *case it may have been the fact that her new husband was a clerk in*

holy orders that led her to marry in her maiden name and describe herself as a 'spinster', but she was certainly not alone in doing so.

Short of following every single ex-spouse from divorce until remarriage or death, we cannot say with certainty how many did remarry—with no requirement for a divorcee to describe him or herself as such on a marriage certificate, the official statistics on divorcees remarrying need to be seen as minimum estimates. Even so, they are illuminating. The Registrar-General's report on marriages solemnized in 1859 noted that three involved divorced men (one of whom had married a widow, the other two spinsters). Four years later there were reported to be 20 marriages involving 11 divorced men and 9 divorced women, while by the second half of the 1870s the numbers had crept into triple figures. Of course, whether this increase represented a rise in the number of divorced persons choosing to remarry, or a rise in the number choosing to describe themselves as divorced when they did so, is difficult to determine.

Given that the annual number of divorces only passed the 1,000 mark during the First World War, it is perhaps unsurprising that remarriages of the divorced accounted for fewer than 1% of all marriages before 1922. After that, however, they climbed steadily throughout the rest of the 1920s and 1930s. The figures also suggest that an increasing *proportion* of divorcees were remarrying: in the second half of the 1920s, just over 58% entered into a new marriage, but in the 1930s this was to rise—to over 64% in the first half of the decade and to over 69% in the second.[†]

The Second World War saw a far more significant rise in the overall number of remarriages, with a more than five-fold increase in the number of both divorced men and women remarrying between 1939 and 1947. Even then, in 1948 remarriages of the divorced only accounted for 7-8% of all marriages, and this percentage was to fall again in the subsequent two decades; it was not until the 1969 reforms came into force that there was a further significant increase, with one in ten of all marriages in 1971 including at least one divorcee, rising to more than one in five by 1980. Remarriage after divorce had come to account for a significant minority of all marriages (see Fig. (i)).

† McGregor, p. 39

When could divorcees remarry?

The simple answer was that it was possible to remarry as soon as the divorce had been finalised. Some individuals, however, made the mistake of assuming that this had happened rather sooner than was in fact the case. The two-stage process of decree nisi and decree absolute was primarily responsible for the confusion:

> *In 1868, Edwin Noble, a Suffolk tailor, petitioned for a divorce. The decree nisi was granted on November 28th, and on December 11th he went through a ceremony of marriage with Rebecca Howes. The following year, the Queen's Proctor brought these facts to the attention of the court. Not only was his marriage to Rebecca void, but Edwin had potentially jeopardised the possibility of obtaining a divorce from his first wife, having, in the eyes of the law, committed adultery, albeit with the woman he thought was his wife. The court was, however, willing to believe his statement that he had assumed that he was free to remarry, and exercised its discretion to make the decree of divorce absolute despite his adultery.*

Who could divorcees remarry?

Unlike other countries, no special restrictions were ever placed on the remarriage of the adulterous spouse. Law-makers pointed out that a ban on remarriage would remove any possibility of redemption—while the more cynical suggested that it might be more of a disincentive to adultery if the divorced spouse were required to marry the co-respondent.

There was, however, one restriction on remarriage after divorce that persisted until the late twentieth century. The prohibition on marriages between former in-laws is well-known, but was almost always discussed from the perspective of the first marriage terminated by death. But exactly the same prohibition applied where the first marriage ended in divorce.

Key Fact: Before April 13th, 1960, a divorced person could not legally marry a former in-law.

In 1859 Alfred Samuel Bacon divorced his wife Elizabeth on account of her adultery with his brother Oliver. Any subsequent marriage between Elizabeth and Oliver would have been void. All three of the parties in fact remarried fairly swiftly to new partners, Oliver in 1860, Alfred in the first half of 1861 and Elizabeth later that year.

Perhaps unsurprisingly, this restriction did not capture the imagination of either reformers or the public in quite the same way. So, when legislation was passed in 1907 allowing a man to marry the sister of his deceased wife, it was specifically provided that a bar remained on remarriage to a former wife's sister where the marriage had ended in divorce. This was the case regardless of who was at fault in the divorce. If the former wife died *after* the divorce, however, it would be lawful for such a marriage to take place.

Key Fact: When in 1907 the law was changed to allow a widower to marry his late wife's sister, a divorcee could still not marry his living ex-wife's sister.

And, as the other prohibitions placed on marrying a former in-law after the death of one's spouse were gradually removed (Table 4.1, p. 186), similar provisions forbidding such marriage post divorce were repeated in each piece of legislation.

Attempts to change the law on the remarriage of divorcees began in the wake of the Second World War, sparked by a number of cases where the law was seen as operating harshly and a perception that this might well be a broader problem in the light of the significant increase in the number of divorces that had taken place. One might imagine that the number wanting to marry the relatives of their former spouse might be small, despite the increase in divorce, but one peer indicated that he was aware of no fewer than 271 couples who would be able to marry were the law to be changed; others speaking in the course of the Parliamentary debates thought that there were many more. And the context of divorce added a new edge to the case for reform: after all, the prohibition seemed particularly unfair where it was the innocent spouse who wanted to marry a former in-law. One of the hard cases produced by reformers included that of a sergeant who had divorced his wife on account of her wartime adultery with a

Polish Air Force Officer; the wife then swiftly married the officer, but the sergeant, who had returned to find her sister mothering his child and duly fallen in love, was unable to formalise his union.

It was also pointed out that those barred from marriage to a former in-law were either travelling overseas to go through the ceremony in a country that permitted such marriages or living together without any ceremony at all. The argument was a familiar one from the nineteenth-century debates over the possibility of a marriage to a deceased wife's sister (see p. 180). Indeed, one of the most intriguing aspects of the debates is how similar the arguments were. There was, on the one hand, the argument that the possibility of marriage might be disruptive to the family circle (although, as one peer pointed out, a man who was so much of a 'blackguard' as to seduce his own sister-in-law would probably do so whether it was possible to marry her or not!). On the other side, reformers used the same argument as their Victorian and Edwardian forbears about the position of children. Given the importance attached to fault in divorce law, the custody of the children of the marriage might be denied to an adulterous wife, and her sister might be an obvious choice as a substitute mother and, in turn, a new wife.

Despite the weakness of the arguments against reform, it was not until 1960 that the law was changed, despite the clear recommendation from the Royal Commission that had examined the law of marriage in the 1950s. In the meantime, the debates did at least serve the purpose of bringing the prohibition to public notice—which inevitably had its downside. One man who had gone through a ceremony of marriage with his former sister-in-law suddenly realised that he was not legally bound by it and apparently 'heaved a sigh of relief, folded up his newspaper and went to live with a barmaid in Bridlington.'

How could divorcees remarry?

The law did not lay down different rules for the remarriages of the divorced:[†] it did not, for example, require any specific period of time

---

† Assuming that the divorce was granted in England: if the country where the divorce was granted imposed restrictions on remarriage, then these had to be respected.

to elapse between divorce and remarriage, nor was any different declaration required. Special provision was however made for marriages according to the rites of the Church of England, while other denominations and faiths were left to decide whether or not they wished to conduct the marriages of the divorced.

Marriages according to the rites of the Church of England

The possibility and likelihood of a divorcee remarrying in the Church of England varied over time. For those divorced by private Act of Parliament (i.e., from the 1660s to 1857) there was nothing to prevent them from getting remarried in church. There was a very good reason for not imposing such a restriction: before 1837, no other route to remarriage would have been open to them. In other words, to have forbidden remarriage in church would have been to prevent remarriage altogether.

Even when civil marriage was introduced in 1837, there was little reason for the Church of England to change its position. For one thing, many churchmen had spoken out against the introduction of civil marriage, and it would have been odd for them to have simultaneously pressed for a measure that would increase the numbers who might have no option except a civil ceremony. For another, the number of divorces remained small, no more than a handful each year. Nor would the legislators have anticipated much overlap between the wealthy men who were the main beneficiaries of the system of Parliamentary divorce and the users of the new civil procedure for marriage, linked as it was to the machinery of the Poor Law.

Key Fact: Before January 1st, 1858, there was no restriction on divorcees remarrying in the Church of England.

So what changed in 1858? The main difference was that divorce moved from being an exceptional remedy granted only by private Act of Parliament to being available, in theory, to all. Many churchmen had fiercely opposed this change when it had been debated in Parliament. Yet at the same time the importance of the religious ceremony was recognised: no less a person than the Lord Chancellor argued that such a ceremony might well render the remarriage 'more sacred' in the eyes of those entering into it. A proposal that the divorced should only be able to remarry in a civil ceremony was defeated, if only by a narrow margin, and in the end the matter was seen as one affecting only the conscience of the individual clergyman. The 1857 Act simply provided that no clergyman of the Church of England could be compelled to solemnise the marriage of any person who had been divorced because of their adultery; it added, however, that any other clergyman entitled to officiate within the diocese could do so. We know from following a number of divorcees through their subsequent lives that there were many who simply denied their divorced status and remarried in church without awkward questions being asked.

Q: *One of my ancestors remarried in the Church of England in the 1860s, claiming to be a spinster and using her maiden name. In fact, she had been divorced by her husband the previous year. Would the marriage have been valid?*

A: While claiming to be a spinster or bachelor when this was not the case would constitute perjury, it did not invalidate the marriage. Using one's maiden name was also unlikely to affect the validity of the marriage: if the marriage were by licence, even using the wrong name would not matter; if it were by banns, there might be questions about what was the right name to use, but if the woman had reverted to her maiden name and was known by that name within the community, then this would be the right name in any case. Even if she had deliberately used a false name, the marriage would still be valid unless *both* spouses knew this was the case and married regardless.

When the law of divorce was again reformed in 1937, and further grounds for divorce were added (pp. 52, 56), a much starker approach was taken. The new law stated that no Anglican clergyman could be compelled to solemnise the marriage of *any* person whose former marriage had been dissolved on any ground and whose former spouse was still living. In other words, it was no longer only the 'guilty' spouse who had committed adultery who could be denied a remarriage in church; even the legally innocent party could also be refused.

An individual's innocence, guilt, or responsibility for the marital breakdown became less important than whether their first spouse was alive. A person who had committed every matrimonial offence in the book and whose broken-hearted spouse had died shortly after obtaining a divorce would be free to remarry in church; yet one whose former spouse had been guilty of multiple adulteries and cruelty would not, so long as the other was still alive. In addition, what had previously been a matter of conscience for individual clergymen now became an institutional one: a clergyman who refused personally to solemnise a marriage involving a person whose former spouse was still living could also refuse to permit the marriage taking place at all in the church or chapel of which he was minister.

The Church of England subsequently reaffirmed its view of remarriage by an Act of Convocation of 1957, stating that marriage, at least in its 'true principle', was 'indissoluble save by death' and that 're-marriage after divorce during the lifetime of a former partner always involves a departure' from that true principle. The then Archbishop of Canterbury went so far as to describe second marriages entered into during the lifetime of the first spouse as 'adulterous'.[†]

Not until the twenty-first century did the official line relax, when in 2002 the General Synod passed a resolution recognising that although marriage should be entered into for life, some unions did fail and that there were 'exceptional circumstances in which a divorced person may be married in church during the lifetime of a former spouse.' Future generations of family historians may begin to find divorced ancestors remarrying in the Church of England from this point, but even today the proportion of divorced persons marrying in the Church of England is smaller than for most other religions and denominations.[‡]

Marriage according to the rites of other religions and denominations

Of course, the fact that only clergymen of the Church of England were specifically exempted from conducting the marriages of the divorced did not mean that other denominations and faiths were compelled to

† McGregor, p. 109
‡ Haskey

solemnise them. Rather, the exemption reflected the special position of the Established church and the obligation on clergymen to conduct the marriages of their parishioners unless specifically exempted from doing so. Other denominations, not subject to any such obligation to members of their congregation, could simply refuse to solemnise a marriage involving a divorced person.

There were, as one might expect, considerable variations in policy and practice. The Roman Catholic church had, and maintains, a clear prohibition on remarrying in church during the lifetime of one's former spouse (although the possibility of annulling the first marriage and thus becoming free to contract a second has been developed).

A number of non-conformist churches proved more welcoming to the divorced. In the early 1950s, only 12% of marriages involving a divorced partner were contracted in a religious ceremony, and of these 87% took place in non-conformist churches.[†] The Methodists accounted for almost half of these, and a case from a little later in the decade shows how in some cases they actively offered to marry divorcees. The couple in question were both regular worshippers at their parish church, but despite this were not only prohibited from marrying there but were also refused Holy Communion for a full six months after their wedding, simply because the groom was divorced. The local Methodist church, however, offered to marry the couple, who gratefully accepted, feeling that it would provide 'the spiritual background both felt would be missing from a register-office ceremony'. By the end of the 1970s, just under half of all marriages in non-conformist places of worship involved at least one divorced partner.

> **Key Fact: If you find a divorced ancestor remarrying in a non-conformist chapel to which they had no affiliation, it might have been because that particular denomination was willing to conduct such remarriages where the Church of England was not.**

† McGregor, p. 117

how long had the adulterous relationship lasted?	when had the adulterous relationship ended?				
	over 10 yrs earlier	over 5 yrs earlier	over 1 yr earlier	during last year	still ongoing
just a 'one-off'	12	15	26	30	-
0-1 yr	3	6	6	14	3
1-5 yrs	-	4	11	7	23
5-10 yrs	-	2	3	3	25
over 10 yrs	-	-	-	-	10
discontinuous	-	2	1	13	14

Table 1.2 *The nature and length of adulterous relationships as recorded in divorce petitions in 1858, when judicial divorce became available.* Note the relatively high proportion of adulterous relationships dating back more than 5 years, the change in the law having enabled spouses to petition for divorce where previously this had not been an option.

how long had the adulterous relationship lasted?	when had the adulterous relationship ended?				
	over 10 yrs earlier	over 5 yrs earlier	over 1 yr earlier	during last year	still ongoing
just a 'one-off'	1	2	21	26	-
0-1 yr	1	-	9	20	24
1-5 yrs	-	1	8	12	25
5-10 yrs	1	-	1	1	7
over 10 yrs	-	-	2	-	9
discontinuous	-	-	2	6	7

Table 1.3 *The changed nature and length of adulterous relationships as recorded in divorce petitions 2-3 years later, in 1860-61.* The proportion of adulterous relationships of shorter duration and more recent date is noticeably higher, once the initial surge of long-term marital breakdowns had passed.

Civil marriage

The majority of people remarrying after a divorce (or at least the majority of those who are open about their divorced status) have always done so in a civil ceremony. Until the mid-1990s, choosing a civil wedding meant the local Register Office and a different set of expectations about how the wedding should be celebrated. One 1964 wedding planner stipulated decisively that 'a bride who has been previously married should not wear white'.[†] It was the increase in divorce coupled with the continuing reluctance of the Church of England to conduct the remarriages of the divorced that led to civil marriages increasing from around one-third in the mid-1960s to over half of all marriages by the second half of the 1970s: in 1972, the year after the Divorce Reform Act came into force, remarriages involving at least one spouse who had been divorced accounted for 22% of all marriages, but 44% of civil marriages.

Who did divorcees remarry?

Those who had successfully freed themselves from an unhappy first marriage might well look for very different characteristics in their second choice. This would certainly seem to have been the case for Henry Cecil, heir to the Earl of Exeter, in choosing a farmer's daughter from a remote Shropshire village for his second wife, in contrast to his wealthy first wife (see p. 80). Half a century later, Anne Brontë was to depict similar considerations governing remarriage after divorce in her 1848 novel *The Tenant of Wildfell Hall*: the cuckolded Lord Lowborough finally divorces his dashing wife and remarries a woman 'widely different from the first' who was 'remarkable neither for beauty, nor wealth, nor brilliant accomplishments' but possessed of 'genuine good sense, unswerving integrity, active piety, warm-hearted benevolence, and a fund of cheerful spirits', which 'combined to render her an excellent mother to the children, and an invaluable wife to his lordship'. Women, too, might well look for very different characteristics in a second spouse:

> *Henrietta Farquharson, whose first experience of marriage had been marked by the persistent adultery of her husband, and her*

† Owen Williams (1964)

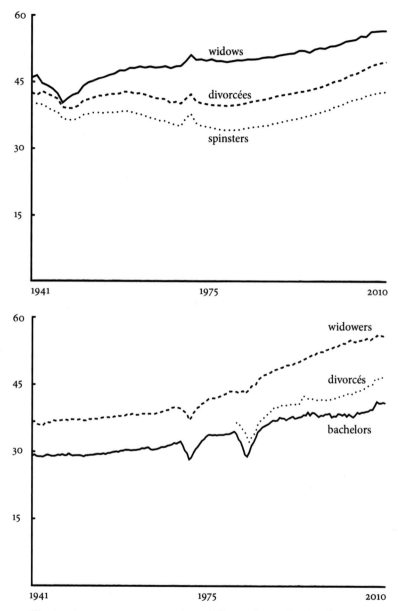

Fig. 1.4 *Average age at remarriage of divorced men (top) and women (bottom) by marital status of spouse, 1941-2010.* Note the post-war decrease, and the rise after the 1969 reforms enabled people whose marriages had already broken down to obtain a divorce and remarry.

infection by him with gonorrhea, understandably took her time before entering into a second marriage. At the time of the 1861 census she was living with her parents in her home village of Hartshorne in Derbyshire; still legally married to her husband at this time, she continued to bear his surname. Although the divorce was granted later that year, a further five years were to elapse before she remarried at the age of 28. Her second husband, 59-year-old Henry Revel Homfray Esquire, of South Place in Stradishall was rather older than her first, and distinctly more respectable.

Given that adultery was the sole ground for divorce before 1937, and that any act of adultery committed by the petitioning spouse might well prevent a divorce being granted, one might suspect that the respondent had a head-start in the remarriage stakes up to this point. Much, however, would depend on the context of the adultery. Was it a regretted one-off, perhaps committed with someone that he or she would never dream of marrying? Or was it a genuine relationship with someone that they would want to marry as soon as they were free to do so?

There were examples of both, but for a more systematic overview we can turn to the parliamentary papers that investigated the first years of judicial divorce after 1857. A diligent civil servant worked his way through all of the petitions up until July 1861 and recorded the dates when the adultery was alleged to have taken place. As one would expect, in the first year of the Act's operation there was a significant proportion of cases where the adultery had first occurred many years earlier; in some cases the adulterous relationship had also been over for some time. In most cases, however, the adultery was relatively recent or continuing and within a couple of years the balance had shifted even further in favour of such cases (Tables 1.2 and 1.3).

Of course, the fact that the adultery was relatively recent does not necessarily mean that the divorced spouse would wish to marry his or her paramour:

Richard Farquharson's multiple adulteries had been committed mainly with prostitutes, and when he remarried after the divorce it was not to any of the women named in his wife's petition. Whether he admitted the truth of his first marriage to her seems unlikely: at the time of his subsequent arrest the story being told by his mother

*was that the first marriage had been entered into when he was only
18, that his first wife had been 'many years his senior' and that the
marriage had been unhappy. The last of these was certainly true,
but Henrietta had been only 21 at the time of their marriage and
Richard a month short of his 20th birthday. The fact that he chose
to enter into this second marriage in his middle name of Archibald
suggests he wanted to hide his true identity.*

How did divorcees describe themselves when they remarried?

It is clear from tracing the post-divorce lives of even a few tens
of individuals that practice varied. Some women used their first
husband's surname when they remarried, some reverted to their
maiden name, and some used a combination of the two. Some
claimed to be spinsters, some widows, and some the ambiguous but
nonetheless telling 'single'. Men too might claim to be either widowers,
bachelors, or single, and might be similarly creative when choosing
what name they wished to record on the marriage register. Many of
these second marriages took place in the Church of England, which
might not have been the case had the earlier divorce been admitted
to.

If you have found an ancestor described as a 'spinster' or 'bachelor'
in the marriage register, this does not preclude the possibility of
an earlier marriage and divorce. Throughout the eighteenth and
nineteenth centuries, however, the one term that should alert the
family historian to the likelihood of an earlier divorce is that of 'single
and unmarried'. It was with this technically correct yet rather euphe-
mistic phrase that the first wife of Henry Cecil described herself when
she married her lover in 1791 after being divorced by Henry; she had
also reverted to her maiden name.

If the remarriage was by licence, then the surviving documentation might well give details of the earlier marriage and divorce:

*Arthur Medworth, intending to marry in his parish church of St
Botolph Bishopsgate in March of 1877, swore on oath that his first
marriage had taken place in 1866, that the decree* nisi *had been
granted on July 17th, 1876, and made absolute just over six months
later, on January 23rd, 1877. A copy of the final divorce decree
was provided, and Arthur also stated that the time for anyone to*

appeal against the decree had passed, leaving him free to remarry.
He would later describe himself as 'single and unmarried' in the
marriage register.

By the 1930s, one finds more explicit statements in the marriage
registers. One wife, remarrying after divorcing her husband on the
basis of his adultery, was careful to describe herself as the 'former
wife' of her ex-husband, 'from whom she obtained a divorce'. When
her ex-husband remarried, by contrast, he was described as 'the
divorced husband' of his former wife.

Did people *want* to remarry after a divorce?

It is clear from the official statistics that remarriages involving one
or more divorced partners became increasingly common over the
course of the twentieth century, accounting for 40% of all marriages
in 1996. This is what one would expect from the rise in the number
of divorces.

One significant change to the *consequences* of remarriage was
made by the passage of the Legitimacy Act in 1959. While legislation
in 1926 had made it possible for children born outside marriage to
be legitimated by the subsequent marriage of their parents, this had
been subject to one important limitation: the parents must have been
free to marry each other at the time the child was born, and if one
or both were married to someone else then this was obviously not
possible. But the perceived significance of the issue of legitimation
led to pressure being placed on judges to speed up divorces so that
couples would be free to marry by the time the child was born, if
only by a very narrow margin. In one case where the divorce was
granted a few hours after the birth of the child (which had occurred
at 7.30am), it was backdated to the start of the day so that the parents
were deemed to be free to marry at the relevant time. The 1959 Act
removed the need for such expedients by allowing the child to be
legitimated even if its parents had not been free to marry at the time
of the divorce.

Key Fact: From December 15th, 1926, to July 28th, 1959, children who had been born illegitimate could be legitimated by their parents' subsequent marriage, but only if they had been free to marry at the time of the birth. After July 29th, 1959, the children could be legitimated even if both parents had been married to others at the time of the birth.

While many long-standing cohabiting relationships were regularised after the 1969 Divorce Reform Act, not all of those who had been living with a partner took the opportunity of regularising an existing relationship. In addition, the huge increase in divorce in 1971 generated a certain wariness: while the overall *number* of divorcees who remarried went up, the *proportion* actually fell quite sharply in the second half of the 1970s. Far more of those who married for a second or subsequent time in the 1970s had lived together beforehand than their counterparts a decade earlier, and the numbers choosing to live together before marrying for the first time also went up. Marriage had ceased to be the only socially acceptable option for couples sharing a home (see also Fig. (i) on the decline in numbers marrying).

In the 21st century, divorce is far more closely correlated with marital breakdown than it was in earlier periods; we have moved from a socio-legal framework where divorce was virtually impossible to obtain to one where over 40% of marriages end in divorce. But what happened to those couples whose marriages broke down in earlier centuries? What were the options available to them, and what were the risks and problems they might encounter? In the next chapter we will look at the different ways in which individuals sought to deal with marital separation that fell short of divorce.

DIVORCED, BIGAMIST, BEREAVED?

❦ **2** ❦

SEPARATED

Given the obstacles to divorce that existed well into the twentieth century, what were the alternative choices faced by men and women whose marriages had broken down? Some, it's clear, simply abandoned their families and disappeared. Others, though, might wish to formalise a separation in some way, or at least come to an agreement with their spouse. The options looked at in this chapter run from the formal legal options that required an application to court, through the detailed separation agreements of the kind entered into by wealthy couples, to the shorter and simpler written agreements of the poorer classes and the practice of 'selling' a wife. Resort was had to all such options long after the passage of the 1857 Act that introduced judicial divorce.

SEPARATION ORDERS

Divorces *a mensa et thoro*, from 1660 to December 31st, 1857

Before 1858, it was the church courts that decided whether or not a couple were married, and, if so, whether they could be expected to live together. Their starting point was that married couples *should* live together, and it was possible for a deserted spouse to obtain an order of the court for 'restitution of conjugal rights', compelling the other to return. It was however recognised that there were circumstances in which spouses should not be expected to remain under the same roof. To this end, the courts also granted orders for separation *a mensa et thoro* (literally 'from bed and board') allowing a couple legally to live apart.

Rather confusingly for historians, these separations from bed and board were also called 'divorces', but they differed from divorces in the modern sense in that did not allow either party to remarry. Indeed, for the church courts any separation was ideally only a temporary arrangement until the couple could be reconciled. The hope was not simply to resolve the dispute between the parties but also to uphold the institution of marriage more generally. As Sir William Scott, who presided over the church court in London, put it in the key case of *Evans v Evans* in 1790:

> The law has said that married persons shall not be legally separated upon the mere disinclination of one or both to cohabit together. The disinclination must be founded upon reasons which the law approves....

The only two grounds on which a separation could be obtained were cruelty and adultery. Most cases were based on adultery alone; a few were based on both grounds. Husbands were more likely than wives to petition the church courts for a separation on the basis of adultery alone; wives were more likely to petition on the basis of cruelty or the two combined, although some did also petition on the basis of adultery alone.[†]

While there is no source of statistics on the overall numbers of separation orders granted by the various church courts across the country, there is evidence to suggest that few were granted, at least outside London. Since one nineteenth-century report calculated that three-quarters of matrimonial cases were being heard in London,[‡] some idea of the numbers involved can be gleaned from the case-load of the London court (Table 2.1). The sharp increase in separation cases in the nineteenth century can be linked to the increase in the number of people seeking a private Act of Parliament to dissolve their marriage, as it was necessary to have obtained a separation *a mensa et thoro* beforehand. But not everybody seeking a formal separation

† Bailey, pp.143-9
‡ Gibson, p. 21

	adultery	cruelty	adultery and cruelty	total
1670-99	47	32	10	89
1701-20	54	43	27	124
1726-35 1746-55	49	16	25	90
1770-99	130	7	16	153
1840-57	186	20	23	229

Table 2.1 *Separation cases at the London Consistory Court, 1670-1857 (after Stone (1990), p. 428)*

order from the church would have wanted (or been able) to proceed to a full Parliamentary divorce—those petitioning on the basis of cruelty rather than adultery, for example, would have had good reason to wish to live apart from their spouse but would not have had grounds for divorce; similarly, a wife might wish to formalise a separation from an adulterous husband but would be highly unlikely to be able to obtain a full divorce (see p. 26). Another good reason for seeking a formal separation order was that the church courts also had the power to order a husband to pay alimony to his wife, at least if she was guiltless of any matrimonial offence. The usual practice was for a wife to be awarded around one-third of her husband's income.

Cost

Of course, to modern eyes the relative rise in the number of cases is less surprising than the fact that there were so few of them, especially given the lack of other legal remedies. Cost was one major obstacle: according to the estimate of one judge in the London church court in 1844, even an unopposed suit would cost at least £50, while one that was contested might cost £800. Others put the potential cost at over £1,000, while Lord Ellenborough was said to have spent £5,000 in his suit against his adulterous wife.[†] Given that even £50 was a large sum at the time (equivalent to somewhere between £4,000 and £146,000

† Stone, p.188

today, depending on how it is calculated), it is little wonder that most genealogists are more likely to find ancestors separating informally than to uncover a separation *a mensa et thoro* in their family tree.

> **Key Fact: Even a separation order from the church courts, while less costly than a Parliamentary divorce, would have been beyond the means of most of the population.**

What had to be proved

So cost was a limiting factor, but there was also the issue of what the plaintiff petitioning for a separation *a mensa et thoro* had to prove. Those accusing their spouse of adultery would need to produce two witnesses—not necessarily ones who had actually caught the unfaithful spouse in the act, but ones who could attest to suspicious activity. Evidence might be given of seeing a couple going into a bedchamber together, hearing the creaks of the bed and panting, and finding stains on the bed linen the following morning. Unsurprisingly, given the class of those involved, it was often servants and chamber-maids who gave such evidence. Proof of adultery might also be established by evidence that one spouse had passed a venereal disease to the other, or, in the case of the wife, by her pregnancy (assuming that the husband could not have been the father). But more circumstantial evidence could also be taken into account, for example if the allegedly unfaithful spouse had been seen kissing or holding hands with another and had had the opportunity to commit adultery.

Spouses relying on cruelty would also have to produce two witnesses, but of course the concept of 'cruelty' was rather more subjective than was adultery! In *Evans v Evans*, Sir William Scott emphasised that the justification for a separation order had to be 'grave and weighty', enough to make it 'an absolute impossibility that the duties of the married life can be discharged':

> Mere austerity of temper, petulance of manners, rudeness of
> language, a want of civil attention and accommodation, even
> occasional sallies of passion, if they do not threaten bodily harm,
> do not amount to legal cruelty....

In such cases, the suffering spouse would simply have to make the best of it. And Sir William's summary of why marriages could not lightly be ended provides us with a lucid vision of the importance which society placed upon the marital contract into which our ancestors entered:

> When people understand that they must live together, except for a very few reasons known to the law, they learn to soften by mutual accommodation that yoke which they know they cannot shake off; they become good husbands and good wives from the necessity of remaining husbands and wives; for necessity is a powerful master in teaching the duties which it imposes. If it were once understood that upon mutual disgust married persons might be legally separated, many couples who now pass through the world with mutual comfort, with attention to their common offspring and to the moral order of civil society, might have been at this moment living in a state of mutual unkindness, in a state of estrangement from their common offspring, and in a state of the most licentious and unreserved immorality. In this case, as in many others, the happiness of some individuals must be sacrificed to the greater and more general good.

It is important, however, not to overstate what had to be proved to obtain a separation on account of cruelty. Though readers will find claims in some histories of the period that only life-threatening acts of violence would suffice, more recent scholarship has shown that the law was not so restrictive,[†] and it is clear that a separation order could be granted where there was a 'reasonable apprehension of bodily hurt'. (It is worth adding here that there has never been a 'rule of thumb' allowing a husband to beat his wife with a stick, so long as it was thinner than his thumb!)

A spouse who wished to contest allegations of adultery or cruelty might simply deny them and produce witnesses to give a different version of events. If he or she could show that the other was also guilty of adultery—a defence known as 'recrimination'—the court would refuse to grant the separation order. Even if the 'innocent' party had been faithful, their petition might be dismissed if they had been cruel or neglectful, if they had connived at the adultery, had

† Bailey

condoned it by taking the faithless spouse back, or had colluded with them over the petition to the court.

> *Henry Cecil's separation* a mensa et thoro *from his wife Emma illustrates the limits of the court's knowledge. Though Henry was petitioning for separation on the basis of Emma's adultery, he had already secretly remarried bigamously! Had the court known, his petition would have failed. In addition, Henry had arguably enabled Emma's affair, allowing her to spend time alone with her lover; and when he discovered the adultery he had inadvertently facilitated Emma's elopement with her lover by taking her to meet him, supposedly to bid farewell. Such acts could easily be interpreted as connivance or condonation. In the event, the court was satisfied of Emma's guilt—chambermaids from inns where she and her lover had stayed were brought forward to testify—and the separation was granted.*

Once the court had decided to grant a separation *a mensa et thoro,* the final necessary step was for the petitioner to promise to abide by its terms and refrain from marrying any other person during the lifetime of the other spouse. Genealogists lucky enough to unearth an ancestor's separation order should take care not to assume that the wording precluded any subsequent remarriage—many of those who did obtain a separation *a mensa et thoro* duly went on to obtain a full divorce by private Act of Parliament.

Judicial separation

January 1st, 1858 to December 31st, 1970

When jurisdiction over matrimonial matters was transferred to the civil courts by the Divorce and Matrimonial Causes Act 1857, orders for separation *a mensa et thoro* became instead orders for judicial separation. The grounds on which such an order could be granted were extended from adultery and cruelty to include desertion for two years. The new civil court, unlike the church courts, also had the power to make orders for the custody of the parties' children and had more extensive powers to award maintenance payments.

Unlike the rising number of petitions for divorce over this period, the number of petitions for judicial separation orders remained relatively static, at around 100 each year. The number of orders granted was lower still, with most never being heard at all. One possibility is that the latter were being settled out of court; a private agreement would, after all, supply most of the practical advantages of a judicial separation but without the potential publicity.[†]

Of course, whether an order for judicial separation was granted or the case settled out of court, the spouses would still remain married to one another and be unable to remarry. For those who had no desire to remarry, or who had moral or religious objections to the idea of ending a marriage, a judicial separation would have been a preferable option. This aspect of judicial separation did, however, begin to attract criticism. In 1912, a Royal Commission pointed out that, because neither spouse was allowed to remarry, they were 'subjected to enforced celibacy', the alternative being 'immorality, and misery to the parties, both the innocent and the guilty.' The eventual solution to this situation was the expansion of the grounds for divorce (see p. 56), rather than changing the nature of judicial separation.

January 1st, 1971 to the present

When the basis for divorce was reformed by legislation in 1969, the grounds on which a judicial separation could be granted were brought into line with the new law. Since the new law came into force, on January 1st, 1971, it has been possible to obtain a judicial separation on the basis of either adultery, unreasonable behaviour, desertion for two years, or separation for either two years (if the spouse consents) or five years (if the spouse does not consent). There are still a modest number of orders for judicial separation made each year, often where the parties have religious objections to divorce but still wish to have formal arrangements for their separation put in place.

SEPARATION IN THE MAGISTRATES' COURTS

Whether or not a spouse sought one of the formal orders described above was ultimately their own decision. By contrast, some might find their matrimonial difficulties exposed to public scrutiny despite their wish to escape attention. A man who deserted his wife and left her dependent on parish relief could find himself brought before the

† Anderson, p. 182

magistrates as a 'rogue and vagabond', facing a potential sentence of three months in prison with hard labour. A woman who deserted her children might face the same charge, but running away from a husband did not incur similar penalties, since she was not legally obliged to maintain him. The assiduousness of parish officials in tracking down absconding husbands can be illustrated by the distances sometimes involved: one, who had left his family in Wigan, was found to be living over 100 miles away in Carlisle; another, tracked down in Hull, was returned to the Norfolk parish 150 miles away where his abandoned family was still residing; a third, from Manchester, was arrested in Dublin.[†]

However, evidence that the wife had committed adultery would lead to the case being dismissed, and some men clearly, if mistakenly, saw this termination of their financial obligations as akin to the termination of their marriage:

> *John Joy, charged with bigamy in 1856, said that he had previously been up before the magistrates for deserting his first wife. Since it had been proved that she 'had been in bed with another man', John had been told that she had no further claim on him, and had interpreted this as permission to remarry. He was told very firmly that he needed a divorce by Act of Parliament if he wanted to marry a second wife.*

Property protection

In addition to providing for a new court to grant divorces (see p. 27), the legislation passed in 1857 also allowed a wife who had been deserted by her husband to obtain an order protecting her property against his future claims. Admittedly, the protection only applied to earnings or other assets that she had acquired *after* being deserted, but it did at least give a remedy to a class of wives who would have been unable to afford the costs of a judicial separation. As soon as the Act came into effect on January 1st, 1858, forsaken wives began to obtain such orders. The Act did, however, have its limits: one early and high-profile case involved a woman who had been deserted by

---

† *Preston Guardian*, May 10, 1851; *Hull Packet & East Riding Times*, March 10, 1854; *Manchester Times*, August 16, 1854

her husband more than five years previously, but who had charitably allowed him to sleep under the same roof as her when he returned destitute; she was held to have condoned his desertion. As *Trewman's Exeter Flying Post* put it: 'Had she been less humane, and closed her doors against the scamp (as he richly deserved), the law would have afforded her relief.'

Domestic violence

Magistrates were also responsible for dealing with violence between husbands and wives, and might well commit a man to prison for beating his wife, or bind the parties to keep the peace. In the late nineteenth century, however, demand grew for a statutory remedy allowing working-class wives to be freed from violent husbands. Legislation passed in 1878 allowed magistrates to grant separation orders to wives whose husbands had been convicted of an aggravated assault upon them. Like a 'judicial separation' granted by the High Court, a separation order granted by magistrates not only permitted the spouses to live separately but also (and even more importantly) could include a requirement that the husband pay a regular sum of money to the wife by way of maintenance. While the Victorian passion for statistics did not extend to calculating the status of those applying for such orders, it is interesting to note that 'the first London husbands separated from their wives by a magistrate's order ranged from a former army officer, a clerk and a bird-stuffer, to painters, porters and labourers.'[†]

Further legislation passed in 1886 meant that a wife who had been deserted by her husband gained the right to seek a financial remedy (as, in 1895, did those who had been forced to leave the matrimonial home on account of their husband's persistent cruelty or his wilfully neglecting to support them). With the maximum weekly maintenance that could be ordered set at £2, these were remedies that catered for a wide cross-section of society. The numbers applying for separation orders casts some light on just how many spouses might have sought a divorce had this been a practical option: by 1898, magistrates were making over 5,000 orders a year,[‡] over ten times the number of divorces granted that same year.

[†] Anderson, p. 171
[‡] Judicial Statistics, England and Wales, 1898 (1900)

But while financial support may have enabled some deserted or ill-treated wives to maintain themselves without resorting to the workhouse, these orders did not enable either spouse to remarry. Wives in receipt of maintenance were likely to have been cautious about forming any new relationship, since by committing adultery they forfeited their right to the money.

Reform was gradual. The Licensing Act 1902 added the 'habitual drunkenness' of the other spouse as a further ground for which separation would be justified and maintenance potentially ordered; this came into force on January 1st, 1903, and was the only ground on which a husband, as well as a wife, could petition. Somewhat later, legislation passed in 1920 allowed magistrates to make orders for the maintenance of children: the maximum was initially set at 10 shillings per child but this was doubled to £1 in 1925.[†] A wife acquired the right to seek a separation order on the basis of her husband's adultery in 1937.

Over the course of the twentieth century the number of such orders increased steadily, and in the aftermath of the two World Wars they increased more sharply (if less dramatically than petitions for divorce: see p. 52). But the balance between separation and divorce was changing: while even into the 1930s there were still twice as many orders being made in the magistrates' courts as there were divorces, after the Second World War the reverse was the case.[‡]

SEPARATION AGREEMENTS

Formal written agreements

Given the attitude of the church courts to separation, and given that they would not endorse collusive arrangements between separating spouses, it is unsurprising that they also took a dim view of separation agreements. Any such agreement to separate would be void as contrary to public policy.

But what if a separating couple wished to engage a lawyer and enter into a formal agreement about maintenance, or about entitlement to the property that each had brought to the marriage?

† Gibson, p.91
‡ McGregor, p. 52

Such issues fell within the remit of the Court of Chancery rather than the church courts, and over the course of the seventeenth and eighteenth centuries it began to uphold the practical terms of separation agreements.

Chancery judges were, however, reluctant to interfere more directly with the jurisdiction of the church courts, with the result that any such arrangements could effectively be undone if one spouse later petitioned for 'restitution of conjugal rights' (see p. 75). Only in the mid-nineteenth century did the House of Lords confirm that, once a separation agreement had been entered into, an injunction could be granted to prevent one spouse from forcing the other to return home. From that point on, there were no longer any doubts as to the validity of such agreements.[†]

For the family historian, the existence of a formal, written separation agreement might come to light in court records if there was litigation over its terms, or alternatively in surviving family papers. Such agreements were, however, relatively rare, since they were only created where a marriage had broken down, neither wished to pursue other remedies, and there was sufficient property at stake to require formal legal arrangements.

Informal written agreements

More common, it would seem, were the less formal types of separation agreement, drafted without the assistance of a lawyer. People entering without legal knowledge or advice into an informal separation agreement might well overestimate what it was possible to achieve. One couple who in 1869 signed a mutual agreement to separate declared in it that their marriage would thereby 'be cancelled and made void for ever', that each would relinquish any claim on the other and would consent to the other remarrying, and that the document 'shall be a sufficient guarantee on the part of each other in any court of law, or before any tribunal whatever'.[‡] The husband subsequently courted a second wife, telling her he was divorced, and went through a ceremony of marriage. Upon his arrest for bigamy he was most indignant, insisting 'I have had a proper divorce, and can prove it.'

† Parker
‡ *Liverpool Mercury*, January 21, 1871

Others chose to vent their feelings in such makeshift documents, with one wife giving her husband what the newspapers described as a 'notice to quit', and telling him that she wanted him to leave, 'for I cannot put up with your grumbling any longer.'

> *Eliza Weaver's first marriage to Thomas Corbett, in 1845, swiftly proved a mistake. Thomas left town soon after, leaving Eliza with her parents, and penned a somewhat tetchy note agreeing to a separation:*
>
> *'I, Thomas Corbett, of the parish of St. Martin's, Worcester, do hereby give up, with a very good will, all claim upon Eliza Corbett and her property and estate, personal as well as real, and advise her to marry again.'*
>
> *Eliza's mother, who witnessed the document, swore on oath that she believed it had indeed freed her daughter, adding that she herself had paid their rent and taxes as Corbett had not. All of those involved acted as if there had been a divorce: Thomas and Eliza remarried, and her new husband accompanied her to her trial for bigamy. Despite the judge telling her that 'she must have been well aware that such a document could not release her from the obligations into which she entered at the altar', the pair remained together (though never legally married) until Eliza's death 36 years later.*

Some written agreements went beyond the fact of the separation and detailed how the spouses' assets would be divided and what arrangements would be made for the children.

> *In 1881, Charles and Isabella Williams entered into a mutual agreement of separation. Charles declared that he was giving Isabella a 'chest of drawers, two chairs, two baths, two bedsteads, a collar box, fire-irons and fender, saucepan, two candlesticks, two tables, all the crockery, and box for knives and forks, washing-stand, jug, and basin, and a chamber' for her own use. It was also agreed that Charles would be responsible for bringing up and educating their eldest child, a boy of four, and that Isabella would not interfere with his schooling. The blend of raw emotion and exaggerated formality is well illustrated by the statement that:*

> *'I, Charles Williams, do hereby declare to not wish to set eyes on Isabella Williams my wife, any more so long as I, Charles Williams, her husband, is alive.'*
>
> *Isabella—described as a 'smart-looking young woman'—then applied to a magistrate to ask if she might marry 'another young man'; the answer, of course, was that the agreement had not dissolved her existing marriage.*

Judging from the advice in newspaper columns, it is clear that readers regularly wrote to inquire as to whether they could legally remarry after separating. *Reynolds's Newspaper*, for example, carried a number of warnings that a separation agreement—whether a 'bond of separation' or a verbal agreement to leave each other 'free for ever', or simply separation by mutual consent—did not constitute a divorce and that either party could be indicted for bigamy if they remarried.

We should not be surprised, though, that couples convinced themselves that such documents had some legitimacy, especially where the agreement had been brokered by their own parents. One young woman, married at just 15 in 1878, soon returned to her parents when her husband failed to support her. His father subsequently wrote to hers to acknowledge the unlikelihood of the pair ever living together again and noting that his son had requested him 'to say that he is quite willing for her to make the best for herself she can, and that he will never attempt any prosecution against her, while he hopes she will allow him to do the same.' In 1881, a man accused of bigamy told the court that his father-in-law had given him leave to get married again, 'upon the condition that he signed a paper, in the presence of a witness, to the effect that his wife was free.'

Separation with permission from the first spouse

In other cases, the agreement between the parties to go their separate ways and remarry if they so wished was even less formal. One young woman accused of bigamy in 1855 told the court that 'My husband is gone for a soldier, and sent me word to do as I'd a mind, and that's the reason I got married again.' Convicted of bigamy, she subsequently returned to her first husband.

The case of Charles Thomson attracted some attention in 1853, when he was tried at the Old Bailey for bigamy. According to one account, his first wife had told his prospective second wife that 'she might have her husband, as she was tired of him, and wanted to have nothing more to do with him.' The second wife, when asked whether she had known the marriage was not legal, said that she had 'thought it was all right' because Charles had told her his first wife 'was nothing to him'. Commenting on the case, Lloyd's Weekly Newspaper *noted 'the significance of this kind of ignorance is not fully understood—it is so profound—so wonderful, it is only with a jerk the mind can bring itself to face it. Yet it is so: people commit bigamy in all innocence—in the parental presence, believing the nuptials to be binding.'*

In this case, it was the second wife who had brought the prosecution, after Charles proved violent. Less sympathy was shown to Thomas Hughes, who in 1891 prosecuted his wife for bigamy after giving her permission to remarry (though admittedly in the rather grudging statement that 'she could do what the damn she liked'). While the judge was forced to find her guilty, he passed no sentence, instead condemning Thomas's cruelty and misconduct and his cold-bloodedness in giving his wife leave to marry and then bringing the prosecution.

'Wife-sale'

One of the more surprising aspects of marital breakdown is the practice of so-called 'wife-sale'. There are a great many documented examples, during the eighteenth and nineteenth centuries especially, of money or some other medium of exchange being given to a husband as consideration for him 'selling' his wife (and, occasionally, their children) to another man. The outward form of the sale could take different guises, varying from relative privacy to raucous spectacle. At a time when the legal processes and costs of formal deeds, court orders, Acts of Parliament, and judicial divorces were beyond the ken of many people and the pockets of most, wife-sale operated essentially as a means of legitimating a *de facto* separation in the eyes of a married couple and of the wider community.

The single best-known example is surely that in Hardy's *The Mayor of Casterbridge*, where Michael Henchard auctions his wife Susan at a fair, accepting five guineas for her from a sailor she has never met. In actual practice, the purchaser seems generally to have been the woman's lover, it having been agreed beforehand that a certain sum would be paid. In 1797, for example, a blacksmith from the Yorkshire town of Cliffe sold his pregnant wife to his workman for two guineas, the newspapers wryly commenting that he had apparently 'sold the child to the *right father!*' If done in public, the sale might serve to give notice to local traders that a husband no longer considered himself liable for his wife's spending. This was made explicit in a case from Bolton in 1831, reported in the *Manchester Times*:

> On Tuesday a monster, in human shape, sold his wife at Tong Moor-gate for 3s. 6d. and a gallon of ale. The purchaser was a brute who lodged in the house. On Wednesday she was delivered up by the husband, according to contract, and on Thursday morning the bellman announced that her husband would not be answerable for any debts which she might in future contract.

A public sale also prevented the husband from suing his wife's lover for damages, as accepting payment quite clearly counted as connivance and fatally undermined any action for 'criminal conversation' (see p. 25). In a few cases, however, the sale seems to have been intended simply to undo the first marriage rather than mark a new relationship, with examples occurring of a man selling his wife to her own relatives. As the *Newcastle Courant* reported on June 16th, 1827, 'At Longtown fair, on Thursday last, Robert Burns sold his wife to her mother for five shillings.'

Because of the desire for at least a degree of publicity, the majority of wife-sales of which a report has survived happened at events such as fairs and cattle markets, or at locations such as a market-cross or a prominent inn. The association with livestock is no doubt behind what is to modern sensibilities a particularly distasteful aspect of the custom: in a significant minority of accounts, the husband is reported as leading his wife by a halter around her neck, as if she were an animal to be sold. In 1825, for example, *Jackson's Oxford Journal* recorded that:

> A journeyman blacksmith recently sold his wife, a decent looking
> woman, with a halter round her neck, at Horsham market, for 2*l.*
> 5*s.*, the purchaser agreeing to take one of their three children!

The price paid varied dramatically: there are reports of wives being
exchanged for as little as 1½*d.*, or a pint of ale, through to amounts
in excess of £150, though the sums involved were more often calculated in pence or shillings than in pounds. More rarely, wives were
exchanged for goods: in 1839, a Lincolnshire tailor was reported to
have accepted a tub of swedes, while the *Bristol Mercury* reported in
1829 that a man had sold his wife for a donkey.

How was the transfer of money understood in such cases? In some
accounts, payment was clearly seen to reflect the value of the wife: in
1810, the *Leeds Mercury* reported that in Hull a wife had been sold for
twenty guineas, noting (perhaps sarcastically) that 'considering the
age of his spouse [this] may be considered a very handsome price.'
Sometimes, the money seems simply to have sealed the deal between
the parties, accompanied by heavy drinking at a local inn; at other
times it looks like extortion: one husband deserted his wife and, after
she had remarried, 'negotiated for her sale, as it were, to the man with
whom she had gone through the form of marriage on the second
occasion'.

In some cases, payment was accompanied by a written document,
duly signed and witnessed:

> This is to certify to all whom it may concern, that I, Thomas
> Harland, of Blackburn, do relinquish all conjugal rights to my
> wife, Sarah Ellen Harland, in favour of Henry Lomax, for the sum
> of £1 sterling.

Occasionally, we find a deed drafted in anticipation of the wife's
remarriage. At her 1856 bigamy trial, Caroline Carter produced a
document signed by her husband John:

> Liverpool, March 3, 1856. This is to certify that I will not appear
> against my wife Caroline Carter, nor from this day forward
> acknowledge her as my wife, or harm or molest her in thought,
> word, or deed, so help me God, for the sum of £10.

The £10 had in fact been supplied by the very same man whom Caroline bigamously married later that day. The judge regarded the agreement as some mitigation, but said that 'it was important that people should know that although a husband might go through such a foolish act as selling his wife, that could not excuse her, or render her the less amenable to the law for an offence of this kind.'

In another case two years later, the wife had been wooed by a man undaunted by her married status. An agreement was subsequently drawn up, whereby her husband was to receive £3/10s., in return for which he signed a document saying that his wife was 'dead to him forever' and dramatically burned their marriage certificate.

In other cases, by contrast, the transaction was less deliberately thought out. One shoemaker, who declared while drinking with a friend that he would 'sell his wife and goods for the sum of one penny', was clearly surprised to be taken at his word and quickly repented of his rash statement. The resulting farcical fracas drew a crowd and eventually the police.

Even if the sale was understood to act as an informal (though legally meaningless) divorce, it does not appear that the purchase was seen as creating any kind of marriage. The reason we know about a number of wife-sales is because one or other of the parties subsequently went through a second formal ceremony of marriage and found themselves prosecuted for bigamy as a result. Those who did not go through a second ceremony of marriage seemed unsure how to describe themselves: the clergyman of Ipstones in Staffordshire described one parishioner as living with his 'bought wife', but in subsequent censuses the pair were not usually given the same surname and the man was variously described as a boarder or lodger.†

And it is clear that, however such transactions were understood by the parties themselves, they had no countenance from the authorities. For a start (and contrary to what genealogists might read elsewhere) a wife was simply not her husband's 'property' for him to sell! A husband who had apparently sold his wife publicly in the market-place in Hull was criticised by the judge 'in the most pointed terms' for his lack of decency. Those men who now and again ended up before the courts directly accused of selling a wife could

† I am grateful to Diane Towers for this information.

find themselves imprisoned for anything up to three months, a clear indication of the official attitude.

As to the prevalence of wife-sale, it is very difficult to arrive at a satisfactory figure. The *19th Century British Library Newspapers* database yields over 120 separate cases in seventy titles across the century, so the actual number must have been higher—but how much higher? A danger in uncovering a considerable number of firm examples of wife-sale is that we jump to the conclusion that these are just the tip of the iceberg, or that it must have been common. Those reporting on them do not seem to have shared this view. One headline in the *Liverpool Mercury* in 1858, for example, screamed 'SHOCKING IMMORALITY: DELIBERATE SALE OF A WIFE BY HER HUSBAND' and described the circumstances as being 'of the most extraordinary character.'

While newspapers did regularly portray the custom as an exceptional occurrence and a barbarous affront to decency, they might also treat it as rather a joke, and public opinion seems to have been similarly varied. In 1859, for example, a Dudley man was reportedly followed through the streets by a crowd repeatedly hooting 'Who sold his wife!' A rumour in the Cornish town of Callington that a man was to sell his wife in the marketplace, on the other hand, seems to have aroused such bad feeling that he feared he might be treated to a ducking by the mob. In 1870, a Bury man sold his wife by public auction to her lover, who then led her away to his home with a rope around her neck. The affair reportedly caused such a scandal that effigies of the husband and wife were burned.

By the final decades of the nineteenth century, it seems to have been assumed that wife-sales were no longer practised. In 1872, the *Leeds Mercury* noted the 'sorry delusion' that had prevailed in parts of Yorkshire that a man could legally sell his wife to another man, adding that 'no one regrets that it has now disappeared, with many other traditional usage and customs no less immoral and objectionable.' Twenty years later, the *Blackburn Standard* expressed surprise upon receiving a question about selling a wife: 'we thought everyone knew that such a transaction is as illegal as it is disgraceful.'

SEPARATION FOR SEVEN YEARS

Finally, it is worth noting the apparently widespread belief that spouses might validly remarry once they had been separated for seven years. Judges across the country referred to this 'popular' but 'idle notion' in dealing with the consequences of such second marriages. There was a degree of truth in such a belief: an absence for seven years would raise the presumption that the other spouse had died (see p. 152) and would also furnish a good defence to a charge of bigamy (see pp. 99, 101 ff). In both of these situations, however, it was essential that there should have been no news of the other spouse during that time: mere separation was not enough.

In addition, if the other spouse did in fact turn out to be alive the second marriage was inescapably void, as the judge emphasized in the 1851 case of *R v Ann Hitchcock*. Ann was acquitted of bigamy on the basis that ten years had elapsed between her separation and her remarriage, nothing having been heard of the first husband in the interim. The judge stressed that, despite her acquittal, the second marriage 'was void to all intents and purposes, and the issue of it illegitimate', and that 'the only instance in which parties, who had once been married, could ever lawfully marry again whilst they were both living, was where the marriage had been absolutely annulled by the sentence of an ecclesiastical court, or by an act of Parliament'.[†]

Despite regular warnings of this kind in court reports and in the advice columns of newspapers, men and women who had been separated from their spouses continued to remarry, although towards the end of the nineteenth century diminishing reports of such cases suggest that the practice was becoming less widespread. There was a clutch of prosecutions for bigamy at Liverpool in the early 1870s, involving a number of couples from Preston, but the Yorkshire newspaper the *Leeds Mercury* took the view that this was a peculiarly Lancashire 'delusion'. This might, of course, have had something to do with traditional county rivalries, for twenty years later we find another convicted bigamist trying to explain to an Irish court that the belief that married people who were seven years separated could marry again was current in the Yorkshire towns of Bradford

---

† *Lloyd's Weekly Newspaper*, March 23, 1851

and Huddersfield! With a certain degree of relish, the Irish judge informed the miscreant that it must be 'a very barbarous country' and 'regretted that the very serious crime of which he had been found guilty arose from superstition through his being brought up in a country so involved in darkness and bewilderment as to the laws of marriage'.[†] The *Huddersfield Daily Chronicle* admitted that cases in the assize courts did suggest a widespread belief in the legitimacy of remarriage, at least where one spouse had not heard of the other for seven years, and that the belief remained despite the best efforts of judges to shake it. It concluded somewhat ruefully that 'it is too much to expect that what our own judges have failed to achieve, an Irish judge will be able to accomplish.'

Of course, the proliferation of possible alternatives to divorce should not lead us to assume that marital breakdown and separation occurred on the same scale as modern divorce. One sociologist, comparing recorded separations at the start of the twentieth century (whether through divorce, judicial separation, or remedies in the magistrates' courts) with the equivalents at its close, calculated that unrecorded separations would have to have been five times higher in the earlier period to match the level of marital breakdown at the end of the century. In the absence of contemporary confirmation of large-scale separation, and in the light of the low proportion of births occurring outside marriage, he rightly concluded that it is implausible that unrecorded separations occurred on such a scale. Had it been the case,

> such unofficial separations would have rapidly accumulated to create a visible pattern of marital upheaval sufficient to create a moral panic within Edwardian society.[‡]

For those who *did* separate, though, the future might be bleak. There was no means of going about a marital separation, short of divorce, that allowed the parties to remarry, but not everyone realised this. Some, of course, may have been indulging in wishful thinking. As the *Leeds Mercury* pointed out:

† *The North-Eastern Daily Gazette*, December 8, 1891
‡ Gibson, pp. 133-4

It is so easy to convince men who have set their minds upon
doing a certain thing that it is lawful to do it, that there need be
no wonder that husbands and wives who wish to re marry before
they are free to do so should yield ready assent to a common,
though very vulgar and absurd, belief.

Others were genuinely confused. As will be clear from this chapter, judges and magistrates would often be faced with a defendant protesting their right to remarry on account of a prior separation, whether formal or informal. Advice columns, too, generally responded with somewhat discouraging news to correspondents hoping to be told they could legally remarry. As *Lloyd's Weekly Newspaper* starkly told one enquirer—who optimistically signed himself 'HOPE'—'No, you would be convicted of bigamy'. And it is to the laws and practices surrounding that particular crime that we shall now turn.

DIVORCED, BIGAMIST, BEREAVED?

3

Bigamist

DEFINING BIGAMY: THE ELEMENTS OF THE CRIME
PROVING THAT THE SECOND 'MARRIAGE' WAS BIGAMOUS
WHY DID PEOPLE COMMIT BIGAMY?
SECOND COURTSHIPS AND CEREMONIES
WHO COMMITTED BIGAMY?
WHAT RISKS WERE BIGAMISTS RUNNING?

Boy: 'Pa, what's a bigamist?'
Father: 'Oh, a man who makes the same mistake twice.'

postcard, 1920s

As we have seen, until the relatively recent past there were a number
of obstacles in the way of obtaining a divorce, particularly if the
spouse who desired one had committed adultery or deserted the
other. So what did people do if divorce was not an option? Did they
simply abandon their first spouse and marry again? If so, how was
this regarded by their friends and family and the wider community?
Were bigamists regarded with sympathy and tolerance, or were they
seen as morally culpable as well as guilty of a crime? In this chapter
we will look first at how the criminal law defined bigamy, then at
what proof of the two marriages would be required, before considering why people committed bigamy, who they were, the risks they
were running, and what happened to them both before and after the
trial.

DEFINING BIGAMY: THE ELEMENTS OF THE CRIME

The history of bigamy is inextricably linked with the history of both
marriage and divorce. By definition, a criminal conviction for bigamy

depends on proof that the accused has gone through a ceremony of marriage with one person while validly married to another; a valid divorce would, of course, free that person to remarry. This might seem obvious, but it is worth restating in the light of the debates as to what constituted a valid marriage—or indeed divorce—for these purposes. We have already seen (pp. 24 ff) just how limited divorce was before the mid-nineteenth century, and it might be imagined that everyone at the time must have been aware of this basic fact. Nonetheless, confusion was generated by the ability of the church courts to grant either an annulment (known as a 'divorce *a vincula matrimonii*', i.e. 'from the bonds of marriage') or a separation order (a 'divorce *a mensa et thoro*', see p. 75). Since an annulment retrospectively wiped out the very existence of a marriage, the parties were both free to remarry (as illustrated in the case of Henry VIII, three of whose marriages were annulled). But the purpose of a separation order was merely to permit a married couple to live apart, and it did not allow either to remarry.

Or did it? In 1552, just as more far-reaching proposals for divorce reform were being considered, the Marquess of Northampton rather jumped the gun and entered into a second marriage after obtaining merely a separation order. An Act of Parliament was subsequently passed to declare that this second marriage was valid, but unfortunately for those concerned the following year saw the accession of the Catholic Mary I and the repeal of this Act. This created a very awkward precedent, whichever way one looked at it: was Northampton's second marriage valid because of the Act of Parliament, or was the Act of Parliament just confirming that it was valid because he had married after obtaining a separation order? If the former, it was another example of those at the top creating laws to suit themselves; if the latter, it surely meant that *anyone* could remarry in this situation. But could anyone rely on their marriages being valid if a new monarch could simply change the rules?

This debate formed the backdrop to the creation of a specific law dealing with bigamy. The church courts had long had the power to declare that a second marriage entered into while the first was still subsisting was void, and to require the guilty party to do penance. But by the start of the seventeenth century firmer measures were thought necessary. We will look first at the elements of the crime of bigamy—and the defences to a charge of bigamy—as set out under the original statute, and then the position after the reform of the law in 1828.

1603 through to June 30th, 1828

At the start of the seventeenth century it was finally confirmed, in the 1602 case of *Rye v Foljambe*, that a separation order (a divorce *a mensa et thoro*) did not give either spouse the right to remarry. The following year, the Bigamy Act was passed, with the unambiguous aim 'to restrain all persons from marriage until their former wives and former husbands be dead.' Even more unambiguous was the stipulation that persons who entered into a second marriage while their first spouse was still alive would 'suffer death as in cases of felony.'

We shall see a little later how often the death penalty was actually imposed. Given the harshness of the potential penalty, it should immediately be pointed out that there were a number of defences, some of which were somewhat ambiguous. The invalidity of the first marriage was one, as was the fact that the individual in question had been 'divorced in the ecclesiastical court'—a phrase that was to generate some discussion. Seven years' absence was, under certain conditions, also a defence, and a particularly important one for those whose spouses had simply disappeared. A final defence was that either of the parties was under the age of consent at the time of the first marriage—which in this context meant 12 for a girl and 14 for a boy.

These were the defences set out in the statute, but others emerged as various issues came before the courts. To understand how the rules applied, it's useful to work through the various situations that might be encountered.

Could a person be convicted of bigamy in England and Wales if they had married overseas?

This depended on whether the overseas marriage was the first or second marriage! The 1603 Bigamy Act referred to the offence being committed by 'persons within his Majesty's dominions of England and Wales.' This was interpreted as meaning that the bigamous second marriage had to take place in England or Wales. So if someone married for the first time in this jurisdiction, and then went through a second ceremony of marriage in France—or even in Ireland or Scotland—they could not be convicted of bigamy by an English court. If, however, they married in France, and went through a second ceremony of marriage in England, they could be.

What if the first spouse died after the second marriage?

The death of the first spouse after the second marriage did not retrospectively validate the second marriage. It did of course mean that the bigamous spouse would be free to contract a subsequent valid marriage: the first marriage having been terminated by death, and the second being void on account of the first, the bigamist would not be 'married' in the eyes of the law and a third marriage would be perfectly valid. Such a third, valid marriage might be to the same person as the bigamous second marriage, or to an entirely different person. If the latter, the bigamist did run the risk of being prosecuted for bigamy by the jilted second spouse.

What if there had been a divorce from the first spouse?

At the time that the Bigamy Act was passed in 1603, there was no way of obtaining a divorce in the modern sense. Later courts puzzled over what Parliament could have meant when it said that persons 'divorced in the ecclesiastical court' would not be guilty of bigamy if they remarried. It was eventually decided that it must have been referring to the divorce *a mensa et thoro*, and the existence of such a separation order therefore became a good defence. In addition, the subsequent development of the procedure of divorce by private Act of Parliament created a new defence: such Acts would explicitly state that the parties to the first marriage could legally remarry, and there was accordingly no question of them being liable to be convicted of bigamy. More difficult was the situation where the remarrying spouse had gone out of the jurisdiction—to Scotland, Ireland, or further afield—to obtain a divorce: the English courts refused to recognise such divorces, and if either party then remarried in England they risked prosecution for bigamy.

How did the defence of seven years' absence work?

This depended on where the other spouse was. It was a defence under the 1603 Bigamy Act if one's husband or wife was 'continually remaining beyond the seas for… seven years together.' It was also a defence if one's husband or wife was absent elsewhere in England and Wales for seven years, if one had not heard from them and did not know that they were living during that time. So in each case there were two elements to be satisfied:

(i) A spouse's absence for seven years *plus* the fact that (s)he was overseas, or

(ii) Absence for seven years *plus* nothing to indicate that (s)he was still living

To give an example of the difference between the two, the simple fact of receiving a letter from the other spouse would negate any defence to a charge of bigamy under the second situation (unless a further seven years' absence then followed) but would have no effect on the first: the bare fact that (s)he had been overseas for seven years would suffice as a defence to a charge of bigamy.

There was also, of course, an important difference between a defence based on a belief that the other spouse was dead and one based on a lack of knowledge that they were living. In the former case it would be very difficult to establish when precisely the belief had arisen: only the most pessimistic of spouses (or, perhaps, the most eager to remarry) would assume their spouse was dead the minute he or she had disappeared. In the latter case there would often be evidence from family and friends to show whether or not the remarrying spouse had heard anything from their vanished spouse during the space of seven years.

What if someone genuinely believed that their first spouse was dead?

During this period, even a genuine belief in the death of the first spouse was no defence to bigamy if the seven years had not elapsed. This rule operated particularly harshly in some cases. One man had received news of his first wife's death and his belief in its truth was shared by her father: nonetheless, as it was later discovered that she was alive and he had remarried within seven years' of her disappearance, the court had no choice but to convict him. Nonetheless, and in defiance of the statute, magistrates might on occasion decide not to send individuals for trial in this situation. This happened but rarely, and usually only where a woman had remarried in the genuine but mistaken belief that her husband had died and also declared her willingness to return to him as her legal spouse (see pp. 137-38).

July 1st, 1828, through to the present day

While the punishment meted out to those convicted of bigamy changed more than once during the two centuries that followed the Bigamy Act (on the changing punishments, see pp. 139 ff), it was not until the early nineteenth century that the actual elements of the crime were changed. As part of a general reform of the criminal law in 1828, three key changes were made.

First, it was stipulated that a person could be convicted of bigamy wherever the second marriage had taken place, as long as they were a British subject. The opportunities for overseas travel were far greater by the nineteenth century than they had been at the start of the seventeenth century, and allowing individuals to escape conviction by marrying in another country had become increasingly anachronistic. Despite this, some individuals clung to the mistaken belief that they were safe from conviction if the marriage had not taken place within England and Wales. More than half a century after the change in the law, a Somerset farmer who had gone through a bigamous ceremony of marriage in Detroit tried to argue that he could not be found guilty in an English assize court. The jury disagreed, instantly returning a verdict of guilty, and he was sentenced to eighteen months in prison. In this case, it should be noted, he had been arrested upon his return to these shores, the laws on extradition being then in their infancy.

> **Key Fact: A British subject could be convicted of bigamy by an English court even if the second marriage had taken place overseas.**

Secondly, the simple defence of seven years' absence where one spouse was overseas was removed: the remarrying spouse would only escape conviction if there was nothing to indicate that the other spouse was alive during that time.

Thirdly, it was clearly stated that it would be a defence if the accused had been 'divorced from the bond of the first marriage': this both recognised the practice that had grown up of granting divorces by private Act of Parliament, and also removed the defence that the parties to the first marriage had been separated by a mere separation order (divorce *a mensa et thoro*, see p. 75).

When a further reform of the criminal law took place in 1861, the section dealing with bigamy was recast in almost exactly the same terms, and this remains the legislation governing bigamy today.

Despite this continuity after 1828 in the law's basic provisions, there were some important developments in the way in which they were interpreted. Firstly, there was a gradual shift in the way in which the courts approached the defence that the first spouse had been absent for at least seven years. The 1850s saw a number of bigamy convictions being quashed on the basis that it had not been proved that the accused knew that their first spouse was alive during that time. And by the 1860s the courts were willing to state explicitly that it was up to the prosecution to show that the accused positively knew that their first spouse was alive during that period. It was also held that the prosecution had to satisfy the jury that the first spouse was in fact alive at the time of the second marriage.

Some absences were far longer than the statutory minimum: Mary Sayer, acquitted of bigamy in 1851, had not heard anything of her first husband for the previous nine years when she remarried, having parted from him 21 years earlier. John Cockcroft's first wife had left only him a few months after their marriage in 1847, and, believing she would never return, he went to America, where he spent the next 20 years. Having heard nothing of his wife in the meantime, he married again in 1871, and the jury had little difficulty in pronouncing him not guilty.

In addition, by the end of the nineteenth century it was not even necessary to prove that the first spouse had been absent for seven years. Over the course of the century increasing weight had come to be placed on whether an individual had actually *intended* to commit a crime (known as *mens rea*, or 'guilty mind'). In the context of bigamy, this led to a new defence in the compelling case of *R v Tolson* in 1889:

> *Mary Tolson's first husband was bound for America, and it was reported that he had been on a ship that went down with all hands. After a decent interval Mary remarried, only to find that her first husband was still alive. The court felt that she had remarried in good faith and it was accordingly held that someone who reasonably believed their first spouse to be dead could not be convicted of bigamy if they remarried within the seven-year period, since they lacked the necessary mental element of the crime.*

Mary Tolson's case did lead to a slight increase in the number of people acquitted on the basis that they believed their first spouse was dead, but it is clear that the courts closely examined whether such a belief was genuine and reasonable in the circumstances. They would, for example, be suspicious of claims based on 'lost' letters apparently giving information of the first spouse's death, and would want evidence that someone else had seen the letter in question. Individuals were also expected to have made enquiries to ascertain whether their spouse had truly departed this life as well as the family home:

> *In 1907, 22-year-old porter Sidney Rayment received particularly short shrift when he claimed that his wife had left him a suicide note saying 'Do not look for Me. I have gone to do away with myself.' His claim to have made enquiries 'for a long time' was slightly undermined by the fact that less than six months had elapsed between his first wife leaving and his second marriage, and his description of himself as a 'bachelor' in the register of that second marriage did not help his credibility. Worse, upon cross-examination he admitted receiving a second letter from his wife, saying 'Sid, I think it now time to let you know that I am still alive, for which no thanks are due to you. I absolutely refuse to live with you any more' and asking for her linen to be sent to her at her mother's house—which, as Sidney acknowledged, 'did not look much like committing suicide.'*

Nor were the courts willing to extend the defence that the remarrying spouse had not intended to commit bigamy to other situations—as those who had obtained a divorce overseas were to find out.

Precisely whether an overseas divorce would be recognised depended to some extent on complex questions relating to domicile. As individuals began to travel the world more easily, rules had to be developed to determine what laws they would be subject to and when. Americans who had been divorced in the US and came to England to remarry would not be regarded as guilty of bigamy, since they had obtained the divorce validly in their home country. But an English man or woman who travelled to the US, obtained a divorce there, and then remarried *would* be guilty of bigamy in the eyes of English law, since the first marriage had not been legally terminated. In other words, it was not possible to escape England's restrictive divorce laws by travelling overseas to a country with more generous provisions, as John Francis Stanley Russell, 2nd Earl Russell, found to his cost in 1901:

> *After his first wife had unsuccessfully tried to annul their marriage, Earl Russell travelled to Nevada and there obtained a divorce. Having publicly announced his second marriage in the pages of* The Times, *he returned home to find himself arrested and duly convicted of bigamy by his peers, and served three months in Pentonville gaol as a result. Earl Russell's first wife promptly obtained a divorce on the basis of his adultery and bigamy, and as soon as he was free to do so he (re)married his second wife, this time validly. Perhaps unsurprisingly, he also became an outspoken advocate of divorce reform!*

As over time the grounds for divorce were widened (pp. 50-57) and the need to travel abroad to seek a divorce was accordingly reduced, so the likelihood was much decreased of an individual being committed for bigamy after divorcing overseas and remarrying.

PROVING THAT THE SECOND 'MARRIAGE' WAS BIGAMOUS

As noted above, the law of bigamy is intimately intertwined with the law of marriage. Proving that the second marriage was bigamous was not merely a matter of showing that the accused had gone through two ceremonies of marriage: if for some reason the first was not valid, then the second would of course not be bigamous. Here two different legal presumptions were in potential conflict: on the one hand, the courts would usually presume that a couple who had gone through a ceremony of marriage and then lived together as man and wife were validly married; on the other, in criminal proceedings, the starting presumption was that the accused was innocent. The courts seem to have resolved this in a typically pragmatic way: clear proof was required that the accused had gone through two ceremonies of marriage, but once this was established the assumption was that the marriages in question had been properly performed. After all, to have required explicit evidence that the banns had been properly called, that the marriage had been celebrated in an appointed building, and so on, would have greatly lengthened what were usually quite simple trials and led to some unwarranted acquittals. And if there was any question as to the validity of the first marriage, those accused of bigamy could generally be relied on to raise it in their defence, in which case it could be investigated.

In this section, then, we will look first at the evidence that was needed to prove that the accused had gone through two ceremonies of marriage, and then sketch out the circumstances in which a marriage might be invalid and so lead to an acquittal.

What evidence was required to prove that two ceremonies had taken place?

Marriages could be proved by a variety of different means. The best form of proof was the actual register of the marriage or a certified copy. Sometimes clergymen were called to give evidence in court and produced the actual register; more often, evidence was given that the copy before the court had been examined against the original register and confirmed as true. A failure to do this, or to have the certificate stamped, would mean that it would not be admitted as evidence.

In addition, there had to be evidence that the person named in the register was the same as the person in the dock. Otherwise, of course, it would have been all too easy for one person to pass themselves off as another for the purposes of the marriage. Witnesses might be called on to identify the accused or their signature in the register, and in a case from 1864 there was an early example of a 'photographic likeness' being used for the purposes of identification. In most cases the question of identity was easily established, but in 1881 there was a high-profile case in which the man accused of bigamy—an evangelical preacher known as 'James Brown, the Converted Clown'—stoutly denied that he was the same person as the 'Henry John Llewellyn' who had entered into a marriage 16 years earlier. He persisted in this defence until the end, but since the prosecution witnesses included his own sister it is unsurprising that the jury did not believe him, and he was duly convicted.

Of course, as family historians will be all too aware, record-keeping was not flawless, and the record of the marriage in question might have been lost or never made in the first place. So a marriage could also be proved by a person who had been present at it, although in this case there also had to be some evidence that the appropriate formalities had been observed, at least sufficient to establish that the ceremony in question was a marriage.

Any person who had been present at the marriage in question could give evidence of its celebration. Often it was the witnesses to the marriage who were called to give evidence: this was more a matter of convenience than a legal requirement, their presence at the marriage being proved by their signatures on the register. Surprisingly, the one person who was *not* permitted to give evidence was the first spouse. Some were most aggrieved to find that they were barred from giving evidence: as one abandoned wife demanded of the magistrates, who else was better placed to know the facts? The simple reason for this restriction was that the law did not permit spouses to give evidence against each other, a limitation that did not change until 1914. The second 'spouse', by contrast, was under no such restriction, since in the eyes of the law they were no spouse at all.

The possibility of a marriage being proved by witnesses was also important where the written record of the marriage was open to question. In the first half of the eighteenth century, a large number of marriages in London were presided over by clergymen operating out of the Rules of the Fleet, an area surrounding the Fleet Prison within which convicted debtors could reside. The scandalous nature of the goings-on at the Fleet Prison, and the unreliability of the registers kept by such clergymen, were constant refrains within the courts. As counsel in one case put it:

> where a Clergyman, un-authorized by Law, shall please to set up, in the Fleet, for himself, and who for Half-a-Crown will put any one's Name in his Register, it would be hard if such a Person or his Register, should have the Sanction of a Court of justice.

The sheer numbers getting married in the Fleet also made it genuinely difficult for clergymen to identify the parties again: these were, after all, people who turned up just to be married, much as in Las Vegas today. As one Fleet parson told the Old Bailey: 'I don't remember faces, 'tis impossible, quite impossible I should remember faces.' In the absence of other witnesses, the bigamous spouse might well escape punishment.

With the passage of the Clandestine Marriages Act in 1753, the trade in marriages in the Fleet came to an end, although the courts were still being asked to determine the consequences of such marriages for some years thereafter. More generally, and as genealogists will be well aware, the 1753 Act had the effect of improving the recording of marriages and may well have made it easier to convict individuals of bigamy: the second half of the eighteenth century saw fewer cases of bigamy at the Old Bailey, but a higher chance of conviction.

Moving into the nineteenth century, the introduction of civil registration in 1837 improved record-keeping still further. And it is clear from the case-law that the marriage certificate assumed a new importance: from then on, spouses were increasingly likely to mention that they had a certificate of their marriage in their possession, and producing documentary proof of the marriages became a much easier matter for the prosecution. The newly appointed superintendent registrars began to make an appearance in the court to give evidence of the marriage, although parish clerks continued to play an important role as witnesses.

Up until 1856, however, those living close to the Scottish border might take advantage of the easier facilities for marriage afforded by Gretna Green and similar 'marriage centres'. The Carlisle Assizes in particular heard a number of bigamy cases in which one or more of the marriages had taken place over the border. After 1856 this trade came to an end, with legislation providing that no marriage could be celebrated in Scotland unless both parties had been resident there for a minimum of 21 days.

What constituted a valid marriage for these purposes?

The accused might, of course, argue that the first ceremony was simply invalid on account of either some technical defect or a more fundamental lack of capacity.

The first marriage might, for example, be void on account of being within the prohibited degrees. Cases did occur where the marriage had been between blood relations: in one case from 1891, the magistrates were faced with a situation where a man had persuaded his niece to marry him and then, when she left him and married another man, sought to prosecute her for bigamy. She was discharged on the basis that her first marriage had been void, and it was clear that the court regarded her uncle as being the one who was really at fault.

More often, the marriage in question was between people related by affinity (for example, a man to his sister-in-law or a woman to her father-in-law). Before August 31st, 1835, such marriages were voidable, and those that had taken place before that date were validated by legislation passed in that year (see p. 179). Such marriages would be valid unless specifically annulled, and so any subsequent marriage during the lifetime of either spouse would be bigamous and void. Any such affine marriages that took place after August 31st, 1835, by contrast, were void, meaning that either party could marry somebody else without committing bigamy. In the second half of the nineteenth century there were a number of cases where men married their deceased wife's sister and then, realising the marriage to be void, repudiated her and married somebody else. In the eyes of the law they were not guilty of bigamy, although such cases added fuel to reformers' campaigns for the law to be changed.

Another possible defence to a charge of bigamy, and one that was put forward in a number of cases, was that the accused's first spouse was already married to someone else when they married them. In such a case, the accused's first marriage would be void, and the second valid rather than bigamous. In some cases the courts had to untangle a whole series of different marriages to work out precisely which were valid, which void, and which bigamous:

In February 1881 William Cox was charged with bigamy, having married Caroline in 1875 and Rosina in 1880. In his defence, evidence was given that Caroline had married George in 1873, which would have made her marriage to William void and his marriage to Rosina valid. But it was then proved that George had also been married before, which would have made his marriage to Caroline void, her marriage to William valid, and William's marriage to Rosina void! At this point the magistrates seem to given up, and simply discharged William, who was to be found living with Rosina at the time of the subsequent census.

Other possible grounds for the nullity of the first marriage (and therefore the validity of the second) were that one of the parties lacked the mental capacity to consent to the marriage, or the physical capacity to consummate it, or, alternatively, that they had not consented to it. None of these reasons loomed particularly large in the case-law on bigamy, although a few defendants tried to argue that the first marriage was against their will, while others had remarried in the erroneous belief that their first marriage was not valid if it had not been consummated.

More significant, at least in terms of the numbers who tried to argue their innocence, was the claim that there had been some technical defect with the first marriage. At this point it will be useful to sketch out the basic requirements of English marriage law over the last four centuries, highlighting those aspects that generated the most litigation in the courts.

1600 through to March 24th, 1754

It has commonly, but mistakenly, been assumed that in this period it was possible to marry by a simple exchange of consent. Historians (and many genealogical textbooks) have accordingly claimed that the consequent flexibility and uncertainty was so great that many people did not know whether they were actually married. Had this been the case, the imposition of the death penalty for bigamy would have been harsh indeed, to say nothing of the practical inconveniences and spiritual dilemmas this situation would have given rise to! (For readers who are interested, *Marriage Law & Practice in the Long*

Eighteenth Century and *Marriage Law for Genealogists* go into detail on this and related points.)

In fact, the case-law on bigamy clearly shows us that the presence of an Anglican clergyman was necessary to create a valid marriage (with the exception of a brief period under the Commonwealth, between 1653 and 1660, when a civil procedure was substituted).

On those rare occasions where the first ceremony had not been conducted by an Anglican clergyman, the accused would generally be acquitted. This was the outcome in one case heard at the Old Bailey in 1738: despite ample proof of both ceremonies, a first wife present in court, and a second wife who had explicitly expressed her resentment and determination to prosecute, the accused was acquitted on the ground that the first ceremony had not been conducted by a minister of the Church of England.

March 25th, 1754 to July 21st, 1822

The Clandestine Marriages Act of 1753 made certain formal requirements essential to the validity of a marriage. Basically, unless the marriage was preceded by banns or the obtaining of a licence, *and* celebrated in church, it would be void. Given that this was the standard mode of marrying even before 1754, this caused little difficulty for most couples, and there are few bigamy cases where the first marriage was declared to be void on account of a failure to comply with the law.

There were, however, cases where those who had married underage by licence escaped conviction for bigamy. Under the 1753 Act, a marriage was void if entered into by a minor (under the age of 21) by licence but without parental consent. In the context of bigamy trials, once the accused had shown that he or she was underage at the time of the wedding, that the marriage was by licence, and there was no record of parental consent, the burden of proof shifted to the prosecutor to show that consent had been given. In one bigamy case from 1802, for example, it was decided that the absence of any statement in the register that the underage groom's father had consented, together with the fact that his parents were not known ever to have visited England, was *prima facie* evidence that the marriage was conducted without consent; the defendant was acquitted.

The acquittals of the young men in such cases would have alerted future prosecutors to the need to provide explicit evidence of parental approval if the first marriage was by licence. But they also created a wider impression that it was possible to go through a second marriage if the first had been entered into while underage, and throughout the nineteenth century people accused of bigamy continued to raise this as an excuse.

Q: *I've found an ancestor who married for the first time when he was just 20 and again—to a different woman—when he was 22! The first wife was still alive, but I can't find any indication that he was tried for bigamy. Which was the legal marriage in this case?*

A: Since he was underage at the time of the first marriage, this would depend on whether it was by banns or by licence. If by banns, then it would be valid (assuming no other impediments!). If by licence, it would depend on whether his parents had consented (either before or after the ceremony). While the church courts would try to uphold a marriage wherever possible unless it had clearly been celebrated without parental consent, the criminal courts would start by presuming the innocence of the accused (and hence the invalidity of the first marriage) unless the contrary was shown.

July 22nd, 1822 to October 30th, 1823

Sometimes, of course, the individuals concerned had good reason to believe that their marriage was invalid, particularly where the law was in a state of flux. Efforts to reform the 1753 Act led to no fewer than three pieces of legislation being passed in the twelve months between July, 1822 and July, 1823. Just to add to the confusion, not only did each of these Acts make provision for a different set of rules to apply for the future, they also contained provisions that applied retrospectively to validate marriages that might otherwise have been void. This was bad news for some bigamists. One young woman who was caught out by the change in the law had married only a couple of days before new legislation was due to come into force; she later found to her cost that her teenage marriage by licence without parental consent was actually valid, and that her second marriage was therefore both invalid and bigamous. The judges, however, felt a considerable degree of sympathy for her and imposed only a nominal punishment.

What is of interest here is not so much the legal framework that governed how couples should marry, but the circumstances in which a marriage might be void—to which a different timetable applied. Given the courts' reluctance to allow individuals to escape conviction for bigamy by using a false name when marrying by banns, the changing rules were primarily of relevance to underage marriages by licence without parental consent. To put it at its simplest, prior to July 22nd, 1822, such marriages were governed by the 1753 Act but would be validated by the retrospective provisions of the 1822 Act if the parties were still living together on that date. Those celebrated between the passage of the 1822 Act on July 22nd and its repeal on March 26th, 1823, would be valid, but the 1753 Act applied with full force to those marriages celebrated between from March 26th until October 30th, 1823. Readers will be forgiven for finding this situation very confusing indeed, and any who have found ancestors whose marriages fall within this period are welcome to get in touch to check their understanding of the laws that applied at any given point (see p. 203).

November 1st, 1823, to the present day

Legislation passed in 1823 made it more difficult to annul a marriage on the basis that the formalities had not been correctly observed. From November 1st, a marriage was only void if both parties had 'knowingly and wilfully' failed to observe the legal requirements. In other words, if *both* bride and groom knew at the time of their marriage that the banns had not been called correctly, then the marriage would be void; if only *one* of them was aware of the problem, the marriage would be valid. This wording was included in the 1836 Act that made provision for civil marriages and those on other religious premises, and in the 1949 Act that constitutes the current law. It is thus rare for a marriage after 1823 to be found void on account of some technical informality.

Was it possible to escape a conviction for bigamy on the basis that the second marriage would have been void anyway?

Bigamy is in one sense a rather curious crime, in that the offence lies in doing something that has no legal effect: if a married person goes through a ceremony of marriage with someone other than their existing spouse, that second ceremony obviously cannot create another valid marriage, since a person cannot be married to two people at the same time. The crime of bigamy, then, is going through a ceremony of marriage while already married to a different person, rather than being married to two people. This then raises the question of whether a person could avoid a conviction for bigamy by arguing that the second ceremony could not in any event have created a valid marriage: if, for example, the second ceremony had been between two people who could not marry because they were within the prohibited degrees. In other words, did it matter if the second marriage would have been void anyway?

One might imagine that the answer would be a straightforward 'no', but there were occasional cases where the court decided that it did matter. In 1791, for example, the public was transfixed by the unexpected acquittal of a man named Thomas Hornby Morland:

> Both of Morland's wives had been present at his trial in the Old Bailey; both, however, had been underage at the time of their marriages and had therefore needed parental consent in order to marry by licence. While consent had been given for the first marriage, the father of the second wife gave evidence that he would not have consented. Morland's counsel, the great defence barrister William Garrow (lately better known through the TV series Garrow's Law), declared that this precluded any conviction for bigamy, and the judge, with evident reluctance, ordered the jury to acquit Morland on the ground that his second marriage had not been valid for lack of parental consent.

The decision understandably caused consternation among the legal profession. The subsequent trend was for the courts to decide that the *theoretical* validity of the second marriage did not matter. In the 1814 case of a husband who adopted a false name for his second, bigamous marriage, the court held that he was rightly convicted of bigamy, even though his alias could have invalidated the marriage. The same approach was adopted in subsequent cases involving marriages by banns, and where the second marriage would have been void as being within the prohibited degrees. This was the verdict in the 1872 case of *R v Allen*: after the death of his first wife, Henry Allen had remarried, but while this second wife was still living he went through a ceremony of marriage with his first wife's niece. In a judgment that was a masterpiece of Victorian moral indignation, the judge declared that bigamy was 'an outrage on public decency and morals' that created 'a public scandal by the prostitution of a solemn ceremony', and that this was the case regardless of whether there was any other impediment to the second marriage.

Now that we know the circumstances in which a person might be convicted of bigamy, we can begin to look in more detail at what the cases can tell us about our ancestors' lives, and a key question has to be: why did people commit bigamy?

WHY DID PEOPLE COMMIT BIGAMY?

There were a wide range of reasons why people went through a second ceremony of marriage. Some were apparently unaware that they were committing bigamy, claiming (with varying degrees of plausibility) that they thought they were free to remarry. Given the complexity of the rules governing when a person was or was not married, we might well have some sympathy for this particular group. Others acknowledged that they had committed the offence but justified their actions by alleging that the first spouse had behaved badly, or that the marriage had simply broken down. Less excusable were those who had entered into the second union as a result of a moment of madness, whether induced by drink or the personal attractions of the second spouse. Most blameworthy of all were those who entered into multiple marriages as part of a career of fraud and exploitation. As we shall see, the courts developed a finely-tuned approach to the relative degree of blame that should attach to the crime in different cases, reflecting this in the sentences handed down. In this section we will be drawing out the nuances of different examples of bigamy to set that in context.

Those who believed that they were entitled to remarry

Some of those accused of bigamy pleaded their innocence on the basis that they thought that the first marriage was either void or had been terminated by the death of, or a divorce from, the first spouse. Some, of course, were duly acquitted, depending on whether the facts of their case fell within the scope of one of the defences outlined above (if, for example, their spouse had been presumed dead and had not been heard of for a sufficient time: see pp. 99, 101). Others, while no doubt genuinely believing in their right to remarry, were convicted, having been caught out by changes in the law, dimly remembered defences, or a failure to appreciate what was actually required for a valid marriage. And there were of course some whose claims of innocence lack all plausibility, and whom one suspects were grasping at straws.

One misunderstanding was that the parties were not bound by a first marriage that had never been consummated. Like many misunderstandings, this had its root in the fact that a marriage could be annulled where either spouse was incapable of consummating it. This, however, had to be proved to the satisfaction of a court (a church court before 1857 and a civil court thereafter). As some brides found to their cost, running away within hours of the first wedding did not render it any less binding, and going through a second ceremony (as some did within days) would expose them to prosecution.

Others pleaded that there had been a problem with the first ceremony, seemingly unaware that a failure to comply with the formalities would only rarely invalidate a marriage. Judges gave short shrift to those who tried to argue that they had assumed a false name when they had married for the first time: so long as the name was the one by which the accused was known in the community, the marriage would be upheld. Very occasionally, however, it was clear that the banns had not been properly called and the court would have to acquit the accused, usually with some reluctance.

When it came to the residential requirements, matters were simpler: it was clear from the legislation that no marriage could be challenged on the basis of non-residence. (One judge commented that if this *were* to invalidate a marriage then three-quarters of all marriages would be vulnerable to attack, and the children illegitimate!) Even more hopeless were those arguments, occasionally heard in the first decade or so after the introduction of civil marriage in 1837, that the accused had thought that marriage in a Register Office was not a 'proper' marriage.

Many people thought that the existence of a separation agreement of some kind would entitle them to remarry. Of course, even a formal separation order would not have entitled them to remarry (although before 1828 it would at least have provided a defence to a subsequent charge of bigamy; see p. 100). But in any case most of the agreements that were produced in court were informal affairs whereby each spouse stated that they released the other from the marriage and would not take any action if the other chose to remarry. The individuals concerned tended to be in a relatively humble station of life and were often genuinely unaware of the law, telling the court (sometimes quite indignantly) that they had obtained a 'regular' separation and so were entitled to remarry.

Another plea that was made on a number of occasions in the early part of the nineteenth century was that the other spouse had been transported. There was, of course, a germ of truth to this: the standard period of transportation was seven years, coincidentally exactly the same period of absence that formed a defence to a charge of bigamy under the 1603 Act. Besides, before the reforms of 1828, if the absent spouse was overseas then it was not even necessary for the one left behind to show that they had not heard from them during that time (see p. 101). The absence of a transported spouse for a period of at least seven years could therefore furnish a defence to bigamy—but only after that period had elapsed, rather than directly upon their convict ship setting sail for Botany Bay!

Finally, there were some people who seemed to think that their own prior conviction for bigamy had dissolved their first marriage and entitled them to remarry. Admittedly, those who made this claim seem to have been somewhat dubious characters: in 1858, for example, a Liverpool warehouseman was arrested for entering into a third marriage, having already served 18 months for his second; his third wife had clearly not shared his view as to his entitlement to remarry, as she had separated from him on discovering that he was already married, and he had subsequently stolen money from her.

Those who believed that they were justified in remarrying

By far the most common reason given for entering into a second marriage was the breakdown of the first. Indeed, in some cases the first marriage had never really got off the ground at all. This was the case for a number of 'parish marriages', where the man had been compelled by the parish authorities to marry the mother of his unborn child but then abandoned her shortly after the wedding.

Other couples had been unable to set up home immediately after the marriage—for example where the husband was in the army, or the wife was a live-in domestic servant, or where their families were unaware of the marriage—and what had been intended as a temporary separation had become a permanent split. Ann Spencer, for example, was separated from her husband two days after their wedding as he was in the army and did not have his commanding officer's permission (see p. 198). The 1873 divorce case of *Charvill v Charvill* also involved a first marriage that had never really had a chance: the bride and groom were both in domestic service, the marriage was a secret one, and the wife had gone abroad with her mistress shortly afterwards. Given that she did not return for nine years, one has a certain degree of sympathy with the fact that the husband had remarried in the meantime. And the divorce case of *Du Terreaux v Du Terreaux* (see p. 36), in which the family and friends of the 16-year-old wife had speedily separated her from her considerably older but socially inferior husband, provides an even more extreme example: the wedding could have taken place no earlier than 8 o'clock in the morning, and by 10 o'clock the girl had already returned home and spent no more time with him.

In other cases, the first marriage had broken down as a result of violence, adultery, or simple incompatibility. Some couples realised very early on in their relationship that they were not suited, and so separated. In one case, for example, the first wife simply told the court: 'We couldn't agree, so I left him'. Another first wife admitted that she had married because she was pregnant by another man. More unexpected still was the 1857 case of a wife-swap in which the parties quickly swapped back! Others repeated their first spouse's parting words by way of justification for their remarriage: one man told the court that his first wife had left him twenty years earlier, 'and said I might go and hang myself, or marry again, and she would never trouble me.'[†]

Most of those who sought to justify their actions gave evidence of bad behaviour on the part of their first spouse, rather than relying on simple incompatibility. There were clear gender differences in what those accused of bigamy saw as justification, with wives more likely to allege brutal treatment on the part of their first husbands. In one case from 1858, a man had been convicted of assaulting his wife, had kept her without food, and had neglected his children, and she had left him and married again. Women who had been deserted by their husbands also often pleaded that they had remarried because they were unable to support themselves. Men, by contrast, were more likely to plead the adultery of their first wife as a justification for their own remarriage. Both men and women were likely to take the view that the remarriage of their first spouse absolved them of any future obligations and allowed them too to remarry.

Of course, bad behaviour on the part of the other spouse was no defence to bigamy, but it might well mitigate the sentence that was handed down by the court, as we shall see (below, pp. 142-44). There were, however, others who had far less cause to abandon their first marriage.

Those guilty of deliberate exploitation

There was a small but significant number of cases where the motivation for going through a second ceremony of marriage seems to have been the property of the second spouse. A witness in the trial of one feisty female bigamist gave evidence that she had said that the man she was planning to marry was only a 'bag of bones', whom she could not love, but that marrying him would mean she could claim one-third of his property when he died and his family 'might go to hell'.[‡] It should also be noted that she was reported as keeping a brothel, which might explain why his family was so opposed to the match. Another bigamist, who received assets of around £3,000 when he married his second wife, was clearly aided and abetted by his first wife, who boldly denied that she was married to him.

† *Birmingham Daily Post*, September 13, 1872
‡ *Bradford Observer*, April 13, 1854

Other bigamists effectively made a career out of fraudulent marriages. One man who, in the words of the *Morning Chronicle* in 1858, had a list of aliases 'which would exhaust the nomenclature of the very thickest of London directories', seems to have been a particularly plausible rogue. Marrying one young woman after a speedy courtship, a few days later he informed her that his business problems made it necessary for him to emigrate to North America. She agreed to accompany him, her money was drawn out of the savings bank, and she went home to tell her family of their plans. When her husband failed in his promise to collect her that evening, she went back to their lodgings, only to find that they had been stripped of every item of furniture which could be removed or converted into money. At his subsequent trial it was rumoured that he had married nearly fifty women.

Such cases were clearly outright scams rather than responses to marital breakdown. But in other cases the distinction was not so clear cut, as financial exploitation might be intermingled with marital breakdown. One man who was tried at the Old Bailey in 1839 blamed his first wife for the time he had spent in the workhouse; his second wife gave evidence that he had spent the £100 she had brought to the marriage: 'he brought me to great destitution, and then left me'; and his third that she had had to give up the good business she had had since knowing him. Overall, cases in which there seemed to be some financial exploitation of a second (or subsequent) spouse accounted for around 10% of those heard at the Old Bailey from 1820 to 1850. (Before 1820 the number of cases is relatively small, making such calculations potentially misleading, while after 1850 the number pleading guilty begins to rise, meaning that the factors relevant to the sentence are not always identified.)

For other men, the motivation for the second marriage seems to have been sexual rather than financial. In the late 1850s, a number of women trooped into the Clerkenwell Police Court to give evidence that they had been married to a man answering to the description of a certain 'Gloucester Gale': each gave the same story of a short period of married life together—ranging from a few weeks to just one day—before he had made the excuse that he needed to 'rejoin his ship'. Into this same category one could also place those cases where the bigamous second marriage seems to have been the equivalent of a brief affair rather than a deliberate decision to end the first marriage. As judges often noted when sentencing male bigamists, the offence could almost be equated to that of rape, since the woman would not have consented to having sex with the accused if she had not thought she was married to him. One can only imagine the feelings of one bride who was abandoned in the early hours of the morning the day after her wedding, when her supposed husband got out of their bed and returned to his first spouse.

Those leading double lives

Sexual and financial exploitation might also play a role in those cases where a bigamist was carrying on a double life—as in the case of the wife of a sailor who took advantage of his absence at sea to find a new husband, while still receiving money from her first, or the husband who took money from one wife to give to another.

> *Employment prospects were the excuse given by Theodore Heldreich for leaving his wife: telling her that he was going to France to look for work, he went instead to Birmingham, where he met a widow with some money, married her, and took her to France with him. Back in Birmingham, he made some excuse for a few days' absence and went to Derby to his first wife, telling her he had got a good job and accounting for the money in his possession by saying it was his master's. He gave her a sovereign, and returned to Birmingham. On his next visit to Derby, however, his luck ran out, as his second wife was informed that he was already married and in 1856 he was duly arrested and convicted. His first wife told the court (one suspects with an air of wearied resignation) that it was the seventh time he had either been married or on the point of marriage.*

More often, however, the impression one gets is that these individuals genuinely had feelings for both spouses or could not face the prospect of ending their relationship with either of them.

Those who remarried in a 'moment of madness'

Finally, there was a small group who seem almost to have committed bigamy on a whim, or in a moment of madness. One young woman told the Liverpool Police Court in 1874 that she had done it for 'a lark', while a number of men proffered the somewhat lame excuse that it had been on a 'drunken spree'. One such example was a sailor about to go to sea, who shared a glass of liquor with the landlady of the Black Bull public house in Sunderland on February 9th, 1852, popped the question on the 11th, and married her by licence on the 12th. More unfortunate—and treated more sympathetically—was the 1874 case of Joseph Creighton, an alcoholic who was shown to be suffering from delirium tremens and who had no recollection of the second marriage: his first wife withdrew the charge of bigamy and he was admitted to the workhouse for treatment.

Others pleaded that they were so infatuated with the second spouse that they scarcely knew what they were doing. This was the case for Philip Field, a businessman in his thirties who fell for an 18-year-old girl. The newspapers subsequently contrasted his 'fine, matronly' first wife with the 'more gaily attired' second 'wife' in a fashionable hat, with a veil hiding 'what was afterwards shown to be a very handsome little face'. In this case, as in many others within this category, there had been no intention of permanently abandoning the first spouse.

SECOND COURTSHIPS AND CEREMONIES

There were many reasons, then, why an ancestor might have wanted to go through a second ceremony of marriage. But how did they go about doing so? Were they honest with the second spouse, or did they present themselves as being free to marry? Were they willing to risk their bigamy becoming known to the community, or did they try to cover their tracks, perhaps by marrying in a church at some distance, or by assuming a false name?

What did bigamists tell their second spouse?

For obvious reasons, exactly what the second spouse knew about their partner was often a matter of some dispute between the parties and received considerable attention in the courts. There were two reasons why this assumed so much importance. The first was the potential impact on the accused. From the early nineteenth century, the courts began to differentiate between different types of bigamy, and those who were thought to have deceived the second spouse into a bigamous and invalid marriage were generally treated more harshly than those who had been upfront with them. As we shall see when we come to look at sentencing patterns (pp. 139 ff), the fact that the second spouse knew that they were entering into a bigamous marriage could make the difference between transportation, or a lengthy period of penal servitude, or a merely nominal sentence (such as a small fine). At the same time, though, the second spouse might have an equally strong reason for claiming that he or she did *not* know of the prior marriage, since people who knowingly entered into a bigamous marriage might find themselves prosecuted for aiding and abetting the bigamist, an offence which potentially carried the same sentence as the bigamy itself.

As a result, there were some unseemly courtroom squabbles as to whether the second spouse had been told of the first marriage or not. Nor was it merely a matter of deciding between the credibility of the bigamist and their second spouse: family, friends, and neighbours might well be drafted in as witnesses. One particularly acrimonious case in 1891 resulted in the second wife arguing with the bigamist's mother, their voices rising to such a pitch that the magistrates had to intervene.

This means that we can be reasonably sure that the proportion of cases in which the court decided that the second spouse had been aware of the first marriage will be fairly accurate. It is clear that some bigamists were entirely honest with their second spouse and told them all of the facts of their unfortunate first marriage before they entered into the second. They were, however, in the minority.

More commonly, people embarking on a bigamous second marriage claimed to be either single, bereaved, or (from the later part of the nineteenth century) divorced. Some second spouses simply trusted their word; others took steps to check their fiancé(e)'s story but were misled by manufactured evidence or by plain lies. One woman who had been duped into a bigamous marriage in Worcester in around 1805 told the court that she had taken 'every prudent step' to ascertain whether her suitor was the widower he claimed to be. He had even shown her the bill for the expenses of his wife's funeral, and the house in which she had died. Unfortunately for all concerned, the wife he had buried was his second—not his first, who was still very much alive. Forging a certificate of divorce might seem like a safer bet: given that divorce remained rare, few people would have seen a genuine one (although there was the additional risk of being prosecuted for forgery if the deception was discovered, as more than one young man found to his cost). And even a *genuine* divorce certificate was not always a guarantee that one's suitor was free to marry: one young woman who had been cited as the co-respondent in a divorce, and subsequently married her lover, later discovered that she was not his second wife but his third, and that the first wife was still living and still married to him.

How was the second marriage celebrated?

The vast majority of bigamous marriages were celebrated in a different location from the first, legal marriage. A few bigamists did risk marrying in the same place, but usually only where the parish was so populous that they were unlikely to be detected. Most preferred to put some distance between the first and second marriages, especially where they had come from a small community.

Before July 1st, 1837, of course, both marriages would have to have taken place according to the rites of the Church of England, save where the spouses were Jewish or Quakers. Once it became possible to marry according to the rites of other denominations, or in a civil ceremony, it is possible to see some interesting patterns emerging as to how bigamists married. Marriage in the Church of England remained the most likely option throughout the nineteenth century, whether an individual was marrying for the first or second time, if only because this was the predominant way of marrying at the time. By contrast, those whose first marriage had been celebrated according to the religious rites of one of the smaller denominations might well chose a different form for their second. One man who was convicted of bigamy in 1881 had married first in an Independent chapel, then in a Presbyterian one, and then in the Church of England, travelling from Cumbria to Lancashire to Essex in order to do so, and adopting an alias for good measure. Others chose a Catholic ceremony for one marriage and a Protestant one for the other. If detected, of course, this chopping and changing might well be taken by the court as evidence that any protestations of innocence were not to be believed. Marriage in a Register Office, by contrast, was noticeably more popular for second marriages than for those embarking on matrimony for the first time, and the proportion of bigamous marriages that took place in a Register Office was significantly higher than the overall rate of civil marriage.

Who attended the second marriage?

Bigamous marriages, as one might expect, were often celebrated quietly and without friends or family being present, and it is possible to get a feel for this from the other names recorded on the marriage certificate. Sometimes the number of guests was so small that two witnesses were literally brought in off the street: one desperate groom paid a passing labourer half a crown to act as a witness when someone else had failed to turn up. The church clerk would often act as a witness to these quieter weddings, and on occasion also acted as 'father' to the bride, giving her away to be married. In one known case, the clerk's daughter also officiated as bridesmaid.

It does of course need to be borne in mind that marriages were generally celebrated far more simply than is the case today: it was apparently nothing out of the ordinary for a clerk's daughter to act as the bridesmaid. Even so, some of those marrying clearly felt the lack of kith and kin. In one example, the bride later told a court that she had given sixpence to her bridesmaid, whose name she did not even know; perhaps understandably jaded by the fact that her marriage had turned out to be bigamous she blamed her 'husband' for not allowing her to have her friends with her. In some cases the very quietness of the ceremony might attract attention if the status of the parties was such that a bigger celebration was expected: the suspicions of one witness to an 1821 marriage were aroused by the fact that the couple had brought no friends with them, despite being obviously respectable and marrying by licence.

On occasion, the relatives of the bigamist were complicit and attended the ceremony, and it is worthwhile closely comparing the names and identities of the witnesses to each one of a known bigamist's marriages. Such cases were understandably rare: one shocked magistrate condemned as 'infamous' the actions of a woman who had officiated as bridesmaid at her own son's bigamous wedding. Even more unusual was the 'father' at one wedding who was responsible for giving away the bride, when she was in fact his wife: as the *Pall Mall Gazette* noted, while it was not always easy to determine who should perform this task, 'it may at least be confidently affirmed that under no circumstances could the lady's present husband properly undertake [it].' The only positive thing the *Gazette* could discern was that 'the peculiarity of the circumstances' must have afforded both men opportunities 'for substituting much novel eloquence for the usual "inexpressive nuptial speech."'

Did bigamists marry in false names?

One of the potential frustrations facing the genealogist with a bigamous ancestor is that bigamists were particularly prone to changing not only their spouses and addresses, but also their names, ages, occupations, and relatives. *The Observer* reported one case of 'a tall well-looking man, of respectable and ready address', who, it appeared, had 'made it a practice for some years past of assuming different characters, for the purpose of entrapping young girls and widows who have been left with small property.' Another bigamist, Henry Bushell, who also went by the names of Dr Bushea (possibly guessable) and Alexander Dingham (a complete concealment), was either lying about his occupation as well as his name or else had a vary varied career: having been a stationer and printer he then became an auctioneer, and afterwards an omnibus driver. Yet another, John Alexander, added the surname 'Short' when he went through his bigamous marriage, also knocking a couple of years off his age and naming his father as 'William Alexander Short' rather than Joseph Alexander. Even when individuals did not deliberately adopt aliases, they might figure with a variety of names in different sources. One man convicted of bigamy in Liverpool in the 1850s appeared in the newspapers as Joseph Malloy, Patrick Malloy, Joseph Patrick, and Joseph Patrick Mulloy, and was addressed by his sister-in-law as simply 'Pat'. Of course, the only reason we know about these aliases is because the bigamy came to light: if it was never detected at the time, it might well be beyond the scope of even the most assiduous genealogist to track down today.

The reports of trials at the Old Bailey provide evidence that around 10% of those accused of bigamy in the 1820s, 1830s and

1840s—usually but not always men—had used an alias of some kind. After that, however, the practice became much rarer, although occasional examples still surfaced. It is possible that the advent of civil registration and the issuing of birth certificates made it much more difficult to get away with using an alias, although of course we do not know how many assumed a new identity and whose bigamous marriage was never detected.

For female bigamists there was a further dilemma: should they revert to their maiden name, use that of their first husband, or adopt some other name entirely? Real-life examples reveal a variety of different practices. Many did indeed revert to their maiden name, although doing so solely for the purpose of the wedding might open them up to an additional prosecution: 42-year-old Mary Cox escaped prosecution for bigamy in 1873 when the court heard that she had believed her first husband to be dead, but the prosecution was allowed an adjournment to consider a charge of 'making a false register of marriage' on the grounds that she had remarried in her maiden name. Some women used the name of their first husband, occasionally added to their maiden name; these included one bigamous widow who reverted to her first husband's name when she left her second and married her third. Others chose a name that would conceal their identity but to which they still had some link, such as their mother's maiden name:

> Abigail Hudson ran away from her Derbyshire home in 1855 to marry her husband's soldier brother, giving a completely false name—'Lucy Bowmer'—despite the unlikelihood of anyone at the ceremony on the Isle of Wight being aware of her identity. Twenty years later, when she married for the third time, she reverted to her maiden name of Winfield, despite the fact that her first husband was still living.

And all bigamists, of course, had to decide how to describe their marital status at the time of the second marriage. As one might expect, individuals opted for whatever was most plausible in the circumstances. Those with children almost always described themselves as a widow or widower, and those who were over the age of 35 at the time of the second marriage were also likely to opt for this description.

Those who were entering into a second marriage at a younger age were more likely to describe themselves as a spinster or bachelor. As ever, though, much depended on the facts of the case and what was known about the individual within the community.

WHO COMMITTED BIGAMY?

Gender

Judging from the records of prosecutions, bigamy was largely a male crime. Men, of course, were more likely to have legitimate reasons for being away from home and thereby having the opportunity to enter into a second, bigamous marriage: there are examples in the case-law of men leading a double life, claiming to each wife that their employment required them to be elsewhere, as well as of soldiers or sailors marrying second wives in the course of their service. It is also worth bearing in mind, though, that men were more likely to be pursued by the parish authorities for failure to support a wife, and bigamy was frequently detected during those enquiries, whereas there were not the same institutional reasons for pursuing an errant wife.

So women always constituted a minority of those accused of bigamy. In the eighteenth century it was a more substantial minority, with women accounting for around 30% of all those accused of bigamy at the Old Bailey in the first half of the century. The 1760s and 1770s saw a slight fall, and by the 1780s and 1790s the figure had more than halved, to around 14%, where it remained (with occasional fluctuations) throughout the nineteenth century. Women did constitute a slightly higher proportion of those convicted at provincial assizes, but still only in the region of 20-25%.

Age

While men and women of all ages committed bigamy, the age-profile largely reflected the role of the crime as a substitute for divorce. In a sample of those tried at the assizes in the 1850s, the youngest to be convicted was a 16-year-old girl and the oldest an 80-year-old man, but the average age at conviction was 34, with the average age at the time of the first marriage being a little over 25 (in line with what one would expect at that time), and the average at the time of the bigamous marriage being a little over 33.

Occupation

Similarly, while examples of bigamists can be found at all levels of society, the vast majority were drawn from the labouring or artisan classes. Again drawing on a sample of those tried at the assizes in the 1850s, we find an attorney, a schoolmaster, a 'so-called gentleman', and various merchants among those convicted; but more common are the skilled craftsmen such as weavers, shoemakers, tailors, and joiners; and even more common are the servants, painters, brick-layers, colliers, brick-makers, stone-masons, and labourers. Some, like the commercial travellers, hawkers, soldiers, and sailors would have been mobile; others, like the shopkeepers—there were grocers, fishmongers, bakers, and brewers—one would imagine to be more static, but in big cities one could attain anonymity within a fairly short distance. Older, more pastoral occupations, such as shepherd, hay-trusser, or drover, rubbed shoulders with the newer, more indus-trial roles of power-loom weaver, engine-fitter, and foundryman. And some bigamists seem to have changed their occupation as often as they changed their name or indeed their spouse: one man was at different times an omnibus driver, a printer, and a 'travelling phrenologist'!

Previous criminal convictions

Bigamists were not, on the whole, serial offenders: the majority had committed no other crimes, or at least none that were unrelated to the bigamy. Bigamy would often, of course, include making false oaths or false entries in the marriage register, the forgery of documents, or perjury, and some bigamists found themselves facing prosecution for these crimes too. A number of husbands were detected precisely because they had deserted a wife and left her dependent on the parish, resulting in steps being taken to track them down. A smaller number were discovered where some violent disagreement—whether between the bigamist and one or other of the spouses, or the spouses themselves—led to inquiries being made. And in a few cases the bigamy was accompanied by some kind of financial exploitation that laid the bigamist open to charges of obtaining money by deception or of theft.

Still fewer, but all the more memorable, were those cases where the individual in question had a rather chequered career, their bigamous marriage being just one element.

> *Philip Walmsley was almost a pantomime Victorian villain, fashionably dressed, with a murky career in the Army, and even a curling black moustache. Married for the first time in 1840, aged just 19, Philip then 'committed an act of dishonesty, was got out of the way and sent to India, where his friends procured a commission for him, upon the understanding that he should not return to England.' However, he fared no better in India, found himself obliged to return, and tried to make his fortune by marrying a wealthy young woman. But suspicions were excited, enquiries made, and the existence of the first Mrs Walmsley and her two children discovered, although not before Philip had managed to squander around £3,000 of his second bride's fortune. He was sentenced to two years' imprisonment, the* Daily News *noting that he seemed 'to be one of those persons who are never happy unless they are getting either themselves or others into scrapes.'*

WHAT RISKS WERE BIGAMISTS RUNNING?

While we will never, for obvious reasons, be able to say with certainty exactly what proportion of bigamists were detected and prosecuted, we can draw reliable inferences by closely examining the circumstances of those who did face justice.

What were the chances of being caught?

Those who ran away from their first spouse with their second were most likely to be traced, since their absence very quickly led to suspicions being raised and inquiries made. In 1805, the landlady of an inn at Rye in Sussex eloped with a soldier after a few days' acquaintance; they departed in a post-chaise and were soon traced to an inn in London, where it was discovered they had married shortly after arriving in the city. Other bigamists took advantage of their first spouse's temporary absence, or tried to get them out of the way, so that they could escape with a new spouse. Annie Clancy, for example, compounded her elopement from her husband in 1857 by taking some of his money with her: when he was away from home for a short while she packed up her clothes, sent them off to York railway station, and there joined her lover. By the time they were arrested, they had already gone through a bigamous ceremony. In 1852, Thomas Barton tried to get his wife out of the way with an excuse about having work to do, so that he could remarry and escape to America. His wife became aware of what was going on, and on the day of the bigamous marriage she told Thomas's new lover. Undeterred, the guilty pair still made their way to Liverpool but were arrested on board ship before it could sail.

More surprising is the speed with which bigamists could still be discovered even in cases where the bigamous marriage had been celebrated long after the parties to the first marriage had ceased to live together. One man, John Harvey, had been separated from his wife for almost twenty years when in 1854 he decided to remarry. But despite going through the bigamous ceremony at some distance from the first, his wife found out and acted so speedily that John was arrested on his wedding night, with a dramatic showdown at an inn in Hereford in which John's new bride (thankful to be still a virgin) became hysterical and his wife fainted.

These were cases in which the bigamous marriage was detected almost immediately, and at the instigation of the first wife. More often, though, it was the second spouse who discovered that the ceremony they had gone through was no marriage at all. A few knew this from the start, but they were very much in the minority. Some, as is apparent from court testimonies, discovered an incriminating letter or, even more damningly, the certificate of the first marriage. On occasion, the bigamy came to light in the course of an argument: Joseph Webb, a watch turner from Lancashire, was so exasperated by his second wife's intemperate habits that he 'threatened to send her about her business, and to bring back his former wife.' The existence of a previous wife was news to her, and she immediately had Joseph arrested. Another bigamist repented of telling his second wife that he was already a married man and claimed that he had merely said so to aggravate her; however, the birth of their child in 1871 seems to have sparked new feelings of guilt: according to the second wife, 'he told me I had a bastard at the side of me, and I was no wife of his, he had a wife in the country better than me.' In other cases it was the return of (or sometimes the bigamist's return to) the first spouse that revealed the deception that had been practised on the second. Such was the story of Absalom Holmes, who served in the militia and, while stationed in Chesterfield in 1855, married a young woman. When his period of service was over he simply went back to his first wife in Bradford; the abandoned second wife 'having her suspicions aroused, first wrote and afterwards came to Bradford, when she ascertained the true state of the case'.

Although in the popular imagination a bigamist is often thought of as having two households at one and the same time, spending time with both and fabricating a network of lies and deception to account for inconsistencies, in actual fact the few bigamists who carried on such a double life rarely managed to do so for long, since their absences from one or other spouse could soon arouse suspicion. William Dixon, for example, absented himself for ten weeks after his honeymoon with his second wife in 1815. Her suspicions aroused, inquiries were made and the existence of the first Mrs Dixon was discovered. Others managed to sustain their double life for a longer period, but eventually their repeated absences led to difficult questions being asked. Sometimes, though, it was sheer chance that led to discovery:

Richard Farquharson (whose infidelity to and divorce by his first wife have already been described: see pp. 28, 68, 70) managed to carry on a double life for some time. Having married Jessie Hooper in 1865, at the time of the 1871 census he was resident in Wiltshire with his mother, wife and young family. Later that year, however, he went through a ceremony of marriage in London with Alice Benest, after a courtship of seven months. For the next two years he moved between the two households: to his London wife he said he had business in the country and to his country wife he said he had business in London. He might have managed to get away with it for longer, had it not been for an incident involving damage to crockery at their furnished lodgings that resulted in an appearance at the county court and a report in the local newspaper. Unfortunately for him, this coincided with a letter from his London wife to the *landlord of an inn at Devizes, where the bigamous Richard had said he could be contacted. The landlord replied that he only knew of one 'Mr Farquharson' and sent her the newspaper report. The mother of his second wife, who seems to have been a redoubtable woman, immediately came down from London.* As the Bristol Mercury *rather gleefully reported: 'a painful scene ensued, and she ordered him to enter the fly waiting at the door, and drove off to the Trowbridge police station, where she gave him into custody on a charge of bigamy.'*

Alongside such examples were ones where the authorities took steps to track down an errant husband. If the abandoned first wife had fallen on hard times and was unable to support herself, the parish would seek out her husband and prosecute him for desertion and failure to support. In the course of so doing, they would discover whether or not he had married again and bring an additional prosecution for bigamy if necessary.

Of course, these examples can only tell us how those cases that made it to court were detected. More telling is the data on where the second marriage was celebrated—or, to be more precise, the distance between the locations of the first and second marriages. If most *detected* bigamists had travelled only a short distance to remarry, then one might suspect a large category of *undetected* bigamists who had travelled further and been more successful in covering their tracks. In fact, most had indeed tried to put some distance between the first and second marriages: in an analysis of cases heard at provincial assizes in the 1850s, the median distance between the two ceremonies was around 20 miles.

In one example where the bigamy was speedily detected, the second marriage had taken place in the Register Office of the Yorkshire parish of Great Driffield, while the first had been celebrated five years earlier in a Baptist chapel in Lincoln (a journey of almost 80 miles). In another, the first marriage had been celebrated in the Tower of London, and the second almost ten years later in Newark-upon-Trent, 125 miles distant. Few bigamists married in the same town, and fewer still in the same place, although in the relative anonymity of, say, London or Manchester some might risk the same church. In other words, these were not bigamies that were, on the face of it, easily discoverable: individuals made efforts to cover their tracks, but were detected nonetheless. Perhaps the most dramatic example of such detection is that of Robert Parker Read, the Somerset-born farmer who travelled to the United States after deserting his first wife and went through a second ceremony of marriage in a private house in Detroit (p. 102). Unfortunately for Robert, his second wife had relatives in Bristol who knew that he was a married man, and who met the newly-weds on their return to these shores to tell her so.

We can also draw inferences from the speed with which bigamous marriages were prosecuted: the shorter the period between the second marriage and prosecution, the swifter its detection must have been. Over half of all of those tried at assizes in 1850s, for example, were being prosecuted within a year of the bigamous marriage. Given that the assizes were only held three times a year, inevitably necessitating some delay between detection and trial, this would indicate that detection of the bigamy had been swift indeed in more than half of cases. A handful managed to get away with a bigamous marriage for more than a decade; interestingly, a number of these were ones who had gone on to marry for a *third* time: perhaps these were more adept at covering their tracks, or perhaps time, distance, and an even more obscure past aided them in escaping detection.

And in the greater anonymity of London it might be easier to get away with a bigamous marriage for longer: of those tried at the Old Bailey in the 1850s, the majority (52%) were still tried within the year, and 81% within five years, but 7% had managed to escape detection for more than a decade.

What were the chances of being prosecuted if discovered?

Detection, of course, did not necessarily lead to prosecution. While in London the police played an increasing role in arresting, questioning, and securing men and women suspected of bigamy from the 1830s onwards (the Metropolitan Police force having been established in 1829), they did not generally take on the role of prosecution. Public prosecutions were possible—and in some particularly egregious cases encouraged—but they were rare. Instead, it was down to the individuals involved to take action. As newspaper advice columns frequently noted, anyone could bring a prosecution for bigamy.

In the majority of cases it was the second spouse who brought the prosecution. Most, it would seem, had been under the impression that they were entering into a lawful marriage, their bigamous partner having usually claimed to be single or a widow(er). Some made their feelings about the deception abundantly clear, telling the court that they were glad to be rid of their spouse, while the *fourth* wife of another bigamist added that she had prosecuted him 'to prevent his repeating the crime with other unsuspecting females'.

But while many second spouses separated from the bigamist immediately and indignantly, not all did so. Some, while unhappy with the situation, continued to live with the bigamist regardless. One second wife told a court that she had learned the truth three years after the marriage, 'but it was never mentioned between them because they could not make the case any better', while a protective second husband declared his willingness to live with his bigamous wife 'to the end of his days.' A few carried their support to the extent of refusing to confirm the fact of the second marriage, although this could land them in trouble, sometimes even leading to their committal to prison until they consented to give evidence. Others separated from the bigamist but decided not to prosecute out of sympathy for their plight or that of the first spouse. Learning that her newly-wed husband was already married, one most forgiving second wife said that he had been an excellent husband during the short time they had been together and that she freely forgave the injury he had done her. Another forbore to prosecute out of consideration for her husband's first wife, who had signed herself as 'broken-hearted' when learning of the bigamy. On the other hand, those who had had less positive experiences of matrimony might also decide not to prosecute simply because they wanted to be free of their bigamous spouse, while some preferred to seek other legal remedies to ensure that they were free, for example by obtaining a decree of nullity.

So there were also a number of reasons why a second spouse might choose not to prosecute, although these might well cease to carry any weight if they found themselves abandoned in turn: one woman, who had known that her husband had another wife for most of the fifteen-year period they were together, only had him arrested for bigamy when he absconded to live with a *third* woman and refused to make provision for her and their children.

Financial considerations might also act as a spur to prosecution: husbands might wish to establish that they would no longer be liable for any debts that their bigamous wives might incur; wives, particularly before the married women's property legislation of the 1870s and 1880s, might want to ensure that their assets were safe from their bigamous husbands. The cessation of financial support might also galvanise a first spouse into prosecuting: the first wife of one bigamist was fairly phlegmatic when she heard he had remarried, but when he stopped sending money for the children she travelled the 260 miles from Kendal to London and 'on account of his still refusing, she had him apprehended.'

If neither of the spouses wished to prosecute, a relative might choose to do so, whether to punish the bigamous party or to rescue the innocent one. This might well happen where the marriage in question was not only bigamous but socially unsuitable. On occasion, however, this tactic misfired, as when the father of the *first* husband of Elizabeth Shields prosecuted her for bigamy on the mistaken assumption that this would dissolve her marriage to his son; the judge convicted her, but had to tell her father-in-law that this only affirmed the validity of her first marriage.

Finally, institutional prosecutions were not uncommon, whether by the parish or by organisations. The parish would usually get involved where the first wife had become dependent on parish funds; often it was the pursuit of the errant husband for desertion that revealed the fact of the bigamy. Other organisations took a role where the bigamist was one particularly deserving of punishment: the Society for the Protection of Females (founded in London in 1835 to save women and girls from the risk of prostitution) took action against a fraudster answering to the name of 'Alexander Borromeo', who was convicted on two counts of bigamy at the Old Bailey, and were warmly commended by the judge for doing so. A similar organisation, the Associate Institution for the Protection of Women, prosecuted the multiple bigamist Gloucester Gale in 1859. Less formal—and rather more self-interested—were the group of men who arranged for the prosecution of James Chadwick in 1846 to test the validity of a marriage to one's deceased wife's sister (see p. 182).

All this makes it clear that a number of conditions had to be fulfilled in order for a bigamist to escape prosecution. The first spouse had to be both unconcerned and, in the case of wives, able to support herself. The second spouse had to be ignorant of the bigamy or willing to live with the bigamist regardless, or happy to give them up to their lawful spouse. Friends, family, and the broader community similarly had to be either ignorant or accepting of the situation. The 1858 case of Philip Field provides a good example of the difficulties in keeping both spouses happy:

Having told his second wife that their marriage was bigamous, but having persuaded her not to prosecute, Philip returned to his first wife. His second then wrote him a letter which was part emotional blackmail and part just plain blackmail, and he decided to leave his first wife for her. When the first wife received his letter informing her that, although she was the one he really loved, he was heading off to America with most of the money from the business and his new wife, she lost little time in reporting him to the police, and he was intercepted, arrested, and swiftly convicted.

Inevitably, then, there would always be a few cases that did not result in a prosecution despite coming to the attention of the authorities. One young woman, ill-treated by her supposed husband, consulted the magistrate when in 1853 she found out that he had a wife and five children already and, crying bitterly, told him that her only wish was to regain what little remained of her property and return to the home of her childhood. In this case the magistrate was able to help her achieve this, although he clearly thought the man should also have been prosecuted. Another magistrate thought an over-eager bride had been as much to blame as the bigamist and, since she only wanted to walk away from the marriage, decided against committing him. In other cases there was a happier outcome; one man who returned from trying to seek his fortune in Australia to find his wife married to another was willing to accede to the magistrate's suggestion of a reconciliation; the second husband, meanwhile, 'disclaimed any intention to rob any man of his lawful better-half, and seemed nothing loth to be quit of his bargain.' A similarly phlegmatic response was evident when in 1854 Jane Constantine's first husband, a seaman, arrived home in Liverpool after a voyage to find that she had remarried in his relatively brief absence. He reportedly told the magistrates: 'if him will have her, me let her go; him no take her me will. Me won't let her starve.'

Such cases were, however, very much in the minority: the vast majority that came before the magistrates resulted in the accused being committed for trial at the assizes.

What were the chances of being convicted?

By the time a case got to the assizes, the chances of conviction were high. After all, the evidence had already been sifted by the magistrates and the fact of the two marriages established. Most of those who had any kind of defence were only too keen to put it to the magistrates as soon as possible and try to ensure their discharge. After all, outside London the assizes were only heard three times each year, and depending on when one was arrested it might be months before the case was heard. Even if bail was granted the period would be one of uncertainty, and if it was not there might be a lengthy stay in prison.

If you have been lucky enough to trace a record of an ancestor's conviction for bigamy you will know that their guilt had been proved to the satisfaction of a court. Even then, how much you will be able to discover about the circumstances of the case varies enormously. Those whose ancestors were tried at the Old Bailey between the late seventeenth century and the early twentieth century should be able to find the transcript of the trial in the published proceedings. While some cases are rich in detail and may provide details of family events and interactions not available elsewhere, others record little more than the dates of the marriages. And where the accused pleaded guilty—an increasingly common practice in the second half of the nineteenth century—little more than the name and sentence is recorded. Some high-profile cases, of course, were reported in both local and national newspapers; those that broke new ground in terms of legal precedent also made it into the law reports and textbooks on criminal law. The downside of such publicity is that the more sensational the case, the more journalists rushed to comment and the more likely it is that some of the reporting will be speculative, highly coloured, or just plain wrong. Run-of-the-mill cases, by contrast, were sometimes not reported at all: it is not uncommon for the report of the assizes in a particular town to note that the cases before the court raised no points of interest and to give no further details! That said, many local newspapers did carry extensive reports of cases heard at the assizes, and more details can often be gleaned from the reports of magistrates' courts. Even if none of these sources yield any results, if your ancestor was convicted of bigamy between 1791 and 1892 you should be able to find them in the digitized Criminal Registers, available on commercial genealogy websites. These give not only the name of the accused and the nature of the crime but also the sentence handed down. While they do not include the reasons for the particular sentence, it may well be possible to make certain inferences about the background circumstances once one knows what kinds of sentences tended to be handed out in what kinds of cases.

What was the likely sentence if found guilty?

In order to understand the risk our ancestors were running in committing the crime of bigamy, we need to know both the *possible* sentence and the *likely* sentence at any given point in time.

Execution

The 1604 Act stated that bigamy was a felony punishable by death, and throughout the seventeenth century both men and women were indeed sentenced to death for the offence. At the same time, a significant proportion were acquitted, and even those found guilty were more likely to be punished in some other way. Men could plead 'benefit of clergy' and have the sentence reduced to branding. While in the middle ages this had been a privilege confined to clerics, after the Reformation it was extended to all who were literate, or at least those able to read from the Bible. The passage often used for the test became known as the 'hanging verse', since knowledge of it would determine one's fate. In one 1677 bigamy trial, Richard Hazlegrove, 'not being able to read, was Condemned and Executed'; it was noted that the case seemed 'a little severe', but 'so the Law directs: which may admonish Parents to bestow, and Children to study at least to read well, since sometimes a man loses his life merely for want of it.'

Women, by contrast, were only given the right to plead benefit of clergy in 1693. That year also marked the last occasion that a bigamist was sentenced to death at the Old Bailey. The accused in this case was a woman who had had a number of short marriages to a long list of husbands: she had stayed with the first only eight days and another just one night. She had also been convicted of bigamy only six months previously. Her claim that she thought this meant that she was entitled to marry again was dismissed, the court taking the view that 'she was an idle kind of a Slut, for she would get what money she could of them, and then run away from them.'

Branding

From then until the mid-eighteenth century, the usual sentence was for bigamists to be branded on the hand. But the severity of this punishment meant that there was still considerable reluctance to convict: before 1750, over half of all those accused of bigamy were acquitted, since the court insisted on the strongest proof of the marriages being provided.

Branding in turn began to fall out of favour in the second half of the century. While in the 1740s all of the bigamists convicted at the Old Bailey had been branded, in the 1750s this fell to three-quarters, and by the 1770s only a couple of bigamists received this sentence. By the 1790s, none of those convicted of bigamy at the Old Bailey suffered branding, although in the provinces occasional cases might still be found—including, in 1791, that of Thomas Hornby Morland, who had acquired a degree of notoriety after being initially acquitted at the Old Bailey on account of the formal invalidity of his *second* marriage (see p. 114). When it was ascertained that there had been an intervening marriage to yet another woman, he was sent to Bury Assizes to stand trial. Upon being convicted, he 'was sentenced to be burnt in the hand, which was done before he left Court, and to be imprisoned twelve months in the Ipswich jail.' The *General Evening Post* went on to report, with some satisfaction, that 'his head is to be shaved, he is to wear the habit of the prison, which is a very disagreeable one, consisting of wooden clogs, &c, and is to be allowed only two hours each day from close confinement'.

Fines and imprisonment

Legislation in 1779 provided that a fine could be substituted—usually just one shilling, although almost invariably accompanied by a period of imprisonment. It is at this point that we find bigamy being treated more humorously in the newspapers—but the humour also has a very distinct gendered edge to it. The *Public Advertiser*, for example, claimed that the punishment for bigamy among the Norwegians 'was that the guilty person should be obliged to live with both wives at once'. The *Morning Post & Gazeteer* quipped that 'those who complain that the punishment inflicted on men guilty of bigamy is too slight, should remember that a Judge, when passing sentence, always gives credit for what the culprit has already suffered', while the *Whitehall Evening Post's* explanation of the slightness of the punishment inflicted was that 'the Court very properly takes into consideration that though the prisoner may have been somewhat of a rogue, he must have been much more of a fool.' And the *Hull Packet* reported the not entirely convincing defence of one man that he had 'forgotten' he was married, and how 'some of our ill-natured satirists say that his first wife must certainly have been dumb, or he would have remembered her for ever.'

Transportation

The development of penal colonies in Australia then opened up a new possibility. In 1795, legislation was passed stating that bigamists could be transported. It is at this point that we see the courts beginning to develop a more nuanced approach to the crime, reflecting the broad range of punishments available. At first this was reflected in the fact that cases deemed less serious were not punished by transportation. The cases that did result in transportation were very varied, including one man who claimed that the separation from his first wife had been consensual and that she had proposed that he 'sell' her at Smithfield market (see p. 88), and another whose first wife had clearly not consented to any separation, and who turned up to claim him back three hours after the second marriage had taken place. By the 1820s, however, the use of transportation had begun to decline, and by the 1840s it was clearly only being ordered in the most egregious cases. The last person to be sentenced to transportation at the Old Bailey was Thomas Constantine Reid, in 1853 (and the sentence in this case seems a trifle ironic, given that he was heading to Australia with his second wife when he was caught!). Not all of those transported in fact ended up in New South Wales or Van Diemen's Land: in 1822 the *Morning Chronicle* reported an inquest on a convict whose sentence of seven years' transportation for bigamy had been commuted to five years' imprisonment in London's Millbank Penitentiary, where he had subsequently died.

Penal servitude

So when the 1861 Offences Against the Person Act substituted a period of seven years' 'penal servitude' (imprisonment with hard labour) as the maximum sentence, in place of transportation, it was merely recognizing that practice had already changed. The maximum was, however, rarely imposed. Indeed, by the final decade of the nineteenth century the most common sentence handed down at the Old Bailey was the virtually nominal one of imprisonment for a week or less.

What factors were taken into account in sentencing?

So what were the factors that were seen as either aggravating or mitigating the offence, and how did they change over time?

The gender of the accused became an increasingly important factor over the course of the nineteenth century, reflecting not only a shift in what the harm of bigamy was thought to be but also changing ideas about female sexuality. In the seventeenth and eighteenth centuries, bigamy had been very much seen as a crime against the institution of marriage: as such, the gender of the offender was generally immaterial. During this period, however, a change occurred in the way that women were perceived: from being seen as the more lustful sex in the seventeenth century, by the end of the eighteenth they had come to be seen as more sexually passive—the rambunctious Moll Flanders of Defoe's 1722 novel had no nineteenth-century equivalent. While the last person to be sentenced to death for bigamy was a woman, during the eighteenth century women were far more likely to be acquitted than were men. In both the 1700s and the 1770s all the women who stood trial for bigamy at the Old Bailey were acquitted, and in between those two decades the proportion varied between 55% and 82%.

Against this new idea of female sexual passivity there then emerged a view that bigamy was more of an offence against the second spouse than against marriage in the abstract. This meant that female bigamists were by virtue of their gender seen as less blameworthy: judges clearly felt that a man who had been duped into a bigamous marriage did not suffer as much as a woman did, particularly if she was young and innocent.

A further corollary of this was that the knowledge and behaviour of the second wife came under scrutiny. If she had known that she was entering into a bigamous marriage the crime was not so great and the sentence correspondingly lighter; similarly, if she had cohabited with or had a child by the bigamist before their 'marriage' then she was not generally seen as suffering any moral harm from the fact that the marriage had turned out to be void.

By contrast, certain factors were always seen as aggravating the crime. Those who had married for financial gain could almost always expect a harsher sentence. So too could those who had engaged in multiple bigamous marriages, or who had already abandoned a second spouse. Deceiving a second spouse was another factor to be taken into account, with those who went so far as to adopt a false name being regarded as particularly deceitful. At least one of these factors was present in almost all of the Old Bailey cases where transportation to Australia was ordered in the 1840s, after it had ceased to be the standard punishment for bigamy, and one bigamist whose case combined all four—financial gain, multiple bigamy, deceit, and a false name—duly received a double sentence. Similarly, when a period of imprisonment was substituted as the mode of punishment, the maximum of seven years was only imposed in a handful of cases, almost invariably ones involving additional marriages or obtaining money by false pretences.

More sympathy was generally shown to those bigamists who had been cheated on or abandoned by their first spouse. From the 1830s to the passage of divorce reform legislation in the 1850s, it was a constant refrain that many of those who committed bigamy did so only because they were unable to obtain a divorce. It was pointed out that Parliamentary divorces effectively licensed those who could afford them to do what would otherwise be a crime: as the *Morning Post* observed in 1851, individuals accused of bigamy might well wonder 'if bigamy be a crime, should these Parliamentary licenses be granted for its commission? and if it be no crime, why am I to suffer imprisonment for it?' Judicial awareness of, and sympathy for, such inequality could well lead to lenient sentences, acquittals, or even discharges without trial.

In the case of female bigamists, spousal violence was increasingly seen as an excuse for entering into a second marriage. The evolution of views on this point is revealing: in 1785, William Garrow sought to defend one female bigamist by proving that her first husband 'treated her in a most brutal manner, and forced her to submit to prostitution to maintain him before he abandoned her.' The court's tart response was 'that might lay her under the necessity of quitting one husband, but could not lay her under the necessity of marrying another', and she was sentenced to be branded. During the first half of the nineteenth century, the sentences awarded to women complaining of violent treatment were not particularly low; but by the second half of the century domestic violence was treated more severely: of the four women alleging violence in the 1890s, two were found not guilty, despite clear proof of the two marriages, while the other two received sentences of four days and one day respectively.

What happened after the trial?

Who did the bigamist live with?

Although it might come as a surprise today, in an age where marital breakdown is more common and readily accepted, in a significant number of cases the bigamist was reunited with their first spouse. This was often the case where he (or more usually she) had genuinely believed their first spouse to be dead when they went through the bigamous second ceremony. As we have seen, in such cases magistrates might be willing to discharge the accused rather than commit them for trial:

> *Ann Burr only learned that her husband George was still alive*
> *when she came to London for a family reunion in 1855 and heard*

his name mentioned. She had last seen him 17 years previously, before he had gone abroad, and she had remarried over a decade later. According to her sister-in-law, she exclaimed 'What! is George alive? I thought he was dead.' Ann left her second husband a year later, allegedly absconding with some £40. He was advised to prosecute her to establish that they had never been validly married. But Ann was acquitted by the Old Bailey because of the length of time that had elapsed between her last seeing her first husband and her bigamous second marriage, and she left the court with her first husband, to whom she had returned.

However, the conjugal rights of the legal spouse were not necessarily upheld by the court. One husband who, 'touching his hat, asked if he was to have his wife back', was given short shrift, the judge being unimpressed by the fact that he had not communicated with her for 13 years. In another case:

John Morgan, who had travelled from Cardiff to London to track down his wife Margaret, might have received more sympathy had it not been for Margaret's own protests that she would never return to him. Upon John denying beating her 'except when I chastised her for taking too much drink', the magistrate demanded why he would want to live with a woman who was a drunkard, had dishonoured him, and who did not want to live with him, and told John he had better go back to Cardiff without her.

One might also find a bigamous ancestor returning to live with their first spouse where the second marriage had been a spur of the moment matter rather than a deliberate repudiation of the first. The infatuated Philip Field, for example, whose story has been alluded to a number of times (see pp. 122, 137), was living in the same house as his first wife at the time of the subsequent census (although she was tellingly described as the head of the household and he merely a visitor!). More surprisingly, perhaps—and disappointingly for those hoping that he would receive his just deserts—the duplicitous Richard Farquharson (pp. 28, 68, 70, 132) was to be found with his legal wife Jessie and an ever-increasing family after serving fifteen months for bigamy.

A return to the first spouse was not, however, always a matter of 'happy ever after':

Ann Wintrip—who had been only 16 at the time of her first marriage and was still only 18 at the time of her second—told the magistrates that she had been persuaded by her relations to marry her first husband and had lived with him only three days 'as she did not care anything about him'. After being twice asked by the magistrates whether she would go to her first husband, she at length reluctantly answered that she would sooner go to him than go to prison. She was then discharged; but left the court with a very sad countenance.

In Ann's case there was clearly family pressure to return to her first spouse, the girl's mother having written to the magistrates to press this course. Where the first marriage had broken down and the second spouse had been aware of the circumstances, it was more likely that the bigamist would remain with the second after the trial, as in the case of Eliza Corbett, whose second husband proved supportive when she was tried for bigamy and remained with her afterwards (see p. 86). A number of other female bigamists had been abandoned and ill-treated by their first spouse and made a conscious choice to remain with their second:

Martha Midgely's first husband had left her 'in a very destitute and emaciated condition' with her body 'covered with sores', having 'driven her out to be a houseless and a homeless wanderer', and had begun to live in adultery with another woman. Martha received only a short sentence at the assizes in 1856—three days—and the following census records her living with her second 'husband'.

Her contemporary Alice Oldershaw also had little incentive to return to her first husband, who had been convicted several times of felony and finally transported to Australia; convinced that he would not return she remarried, but unfortunately he did, and prosecuted her for bigamy. She too served a short sentence and subsequent censuses show her living with her second 'husband'.

Some, then, simply accepted the invalidity of their marriage as the necessary price to pay to be with the person they loved. Others remarried when they could do so legally (thus giving rise to some of those double marriages to the same person which might look puzzling without a knowledge of the intervening facts: see Ch. 5).

But remaining with the second spouse was not always an option. Some clearly had no desire to remain with someone who had deceived them. One aggrieved second wife, upon learning that her 'husband' was still married, wrote to him to say that she intended to seek out his first wife 'and together we will hunt you down', adding, with perhaps pardonable spite, 'I do not mind this half so much as if I were your legal wife; believe me I shall not break my heart.'

While the courts often dwelt on the harm that an invalid marriage might do to the innocent spouse's reputation—'humbling her in the sight of men', according to one judge, and ruining her chances of entering into a valid marriage in the view of another—the wronged second spouse not infrequently married again, sometimes quite quickly:

> *Lydia Vaughan was accused of being vindictive when she prosecuted her husband John for bigamy in 1852, although since he had not only deceived her about being free to marry but had also been violent towards her, one might forgive her. Lydia herself was cross-examined about her acquaintance with a Mr Shepherd, of Bristol, but denied that any 'improper intimacy' existed between them. Two years later, however, Lydia and an Edward Sheppard were wed, and the 1861 census finds them heading a family blending children from their former marriages with their own young daughter. John Vaughan, by contrast, was living alone in Birmingham.*

Of course, without knowledge of the invalidity of the first marriage, a genealogist finding an ancestor going through two ceremonies of marriage with different people might wrongly infer that they were the one who had committed bigamy. In such cases it is always worth further investigating the first spouse, to see whether there was a trial for bigamy or evidence of a prior marriage.

Those bigamists who had no desire to return to their first spouse and no opportunity to return to their second might risk a further prosecution for bigamy by going through a *third* ceremony of marriage with a new partner. One man who was sentenced to four months for bigamy at the Old Bailey in 1853 had been separated from his first wife for over a decade and had no likelihood of returning to his second, to whom he had been particularly violent; he celebrated a third and longer-lasting (though still bigamous) marriage in 1858.

The even more uxorious James Egersdorff, who had contracted two bigamous marriages before his trial at the Old Bailey, went on to marry a *fourth* wife a few years afterwards. Others, if only a minority, decided not to risk a further conviction for bigamy and simply cohabited with a new partner.

Readers with bigamous ancestors should be able to infer a considerable amount about their behaviour and motivations from the sentence handed down by the court and indeed their subsequent actions. On the other hand, those who have discovered an ancestor who went through a second ceremony of marriage during the lifetime of their first spouse but who was *not* prosecuted may need to speculate on the causes. Was the fact of the bigamy unknown to both the first and the second spouse, and indeed to the broader family and community? Or was it known and accepted, in default of any other ways of ending the first relationship? While the process of tracking cohorts of couples through successive censuses does not suggest any large-scale resort to bigamy as a response to relationship breakdown, I would very much welcome evidence of any hitherto undetected bigamies uncovered by diligent genealogists, and will feed this evidence into an upcoming book.

We have also seen in this chapter that many individuals committed bigamy inadvertently over the centuries, believing that their first spouse had died and that they were free to marry again. Those cases that found their way to the criminal courts were those where the first spouse had turned up, but what about those cases where he or she was never heard of again? This takes us on to our next topic, that of remarriage after bereavement, whether actual or presumed....

4

BEREAVED

'The idea of two people spending their lives together was invented by people who were lucky to make it to thirty without being eaten by dinosaurs.'

Kevin Dolenz, *St Elmo's Fire* (1985)

In 1782, Essex Hartop and his wife Elizabeth were living together in the Bedfordshire parish of Cardington with their four children, having married almost twenty years earlier. The household also contained Elizabeth's two adult daughters from her previous marriage to William Urine. William had himself been a widower when he married Elizabeth in 1755, his first wife Ann having died in 1747. Elizabeth subsequently died in 1789, at the age of 53, and it seems likely that Essex Hartop went on to remarry in 1794. As any genealogist will know, multiple marriages like this can prove a challenge when trying to work out one's family tree. But just how common was it for any individual to marry for a second or third time after a first spouse had died? What were the factors that might influence the likelihood of remarrying? Whom, and how, did the bereaved remarry?

ESTABLISHING THE DEATH OF A SPOUSE

Had the first spouse died? This is an obvious question to ask when considering the remarriage of someone claiming to be a widow or widower; and in the usual run of things there would have been little doubt about the matter at the time. But the uncertainties that could arise for our ancestors when opportunities for nationwide and even global travel were outstripping traditional means of correspondence are amply illustrated by the case of Catherine Exley:

> Catherine Exley accompanied her soldier husband Joshua to Portugal when he was fighting in the Peninsular War. But after one battle she was told he had been shot dead, and so she spent a mournful three days searching the battlefield for his body. The soldiers' corpses, though, proved so discoloured and mutilated as to be almost unrecognisable, and she was not certain that the body of the corporal she had found was her husband. Nevertheless, she was treated as a widow by the army and travelled back to England. Back home in Batley, however, a letter awaited her from Joshua: over a year after he was reported dead she discovered that he had been taken prisoner and was in fact alive and well in France.

In this case the pair were happily reunited, but many other women—less cautious perhaps, or more ready to move on after bereavement, or simply in need of support—remarried in the belief that their first husband was dead, only to find at a later stage that this was not the case. Of course, husbands too might find themselves in a similar predicament but, given the greater opportunities for men to travel, it was generally wives who were waiting for news of an absent spouse rather than the other way round.

But what if the individual in question had been absent from home—perhaps seeking work, or having abandoned their spouse—and news of their death only filtered back some time later? Could their spouse remarry? And what if they were simply never heard of again? When, if ever, would it be safe to assume that they had died? The answers to these questions differ according to whether the spouse was actually dead, thought to be dead, or turned up alive and well; depending on the timing of such events, the remaining spouse's remarriage might be valid or void, and possibly bigamous.

Occasionally, we find a person remarrying giving their status as widow or widower, but no corresponding death for the first spouse can be found. While the assumption ought to be that they were telling the truth and that it is the sources that are deficient, it is worth noting that people intending to marry were not, it seems, required to give proof of identity or status—looking at the legislation, it appears that a lot of faith was placed in the parties' own declarations. It was not until the Immigration and Asylum Act 1999 amended the Marriage Act 1949 that a registrar had the power to request additional evidence as to name, age, marital status, or nationality. Earlier generations of registrars must presumably have had suspicions on occasion and asked questions, but it is only very recently that this has been formalised. Given the number who managed to marry bigamously in earlier generations, it's clear that a lot was taken on trust.

Actually dead

If one spouse had died before their spouse's remarriage took place, then that remarriage would always be valid (assuming there was no other legal impediment). Even if one spouse had been uncertain as to whether or not the other was dead when saying 'I do' for a second time—or even of they positively believed them to be alive—there was no question of them being prosecuted for bigamy if the other was in fact dead.

Thought or likely to be dead

If there was simply no news of the first spouse, then the courts might well presume that the second marriage was valid if it felt that it was more likely than not that the first spouse had died before it had taken place. In one particular case from 1819, where a woman's husband had enlisted as a soldier, gone abroad on foreign service, and never been heard of since, the validity of her second marriage was assumed, even though it was only a year after his departure. By contrast, where a man's first wife had clearly been alive 25 days before his second marriage, the court decided that it could not be presumed that she had died in the interim.

As the judges in the case explained, it all came down to the evidence rather than any rigid rule of law. So, for example, different inferences would be drawn if the last letter received from a spouse had announced that they had been seized with a disease likely to prove fatal in a very short time, as opposed to one declaring that they were in good health. In addition, by the early nineteenth century the courts had developed a presumption that an individual who had not been heard of for seven years could be presumed to be dead. So in the absence of anything suggesting death from accident or illness, the mere fact of a prolonged absence might also be taken as sufficient to raise a presumption of the person's demise.

Turned out to be alive

If a person's first spouse turned up alive and well after a remarriage, however, matters changed. For a start, the second marriage would automatically be void. Depending on when it was entered into, it might also be bigamous. The defences to bigamy are dealt with in more detail elsewhere (see pp. 99 ff); for present purposes it is sufficient to note that the remarrying spouse could be found guilty of bigamy unless there had been no news of the first spouse for at least seven years. (It is worth pointing out that an absent spouse need not have reappeared in person—the evidence of witnesses, letters, and so on could suffice to prove they were still alive.)

Some spouses, it is fair to say, remarried with incautious haste. One young woman, Jane Constantine, jumped to the conclusion that her first husband had died: reading an account in the newspapers that the ship in which he had sailed had been wrecked, and one man drowned, she concluded that it must be him. The *Liverpool Mercury* noted rather sardonically that 'the wish, perhaps, was father to the thought, for she at once began to look about for another lord.' Within a few weeks of her second marriage her first husband had returned and she found herself charged with bigamy (for the sequel to Jane's story, see p. 138).

Others though were encouraged to act with caution even once the statutory seven years had passed. In 1881, the *Morning Post* reported the case of a young woman whose husband had deserted her and who had heard nothing from him for the past eight years. She had come to London's Bow Street magistrates' court to seek advice on the legality of remarrying. Having learnt that her only reason for supposing her first husband to be dead was his continued absence, she was advised that further inquiries should be made both of his relatives and those involved in the same trade, and that an advertisement should be placed in the newspapers.

Such advice correctly highlighted the fact that a marriage would not be legal if one's first spouse was still living, however long the separation had been, and that it would therefore be sensible to take all possible opportunities to ascertain whether he or she was alive or dead. The difference between a marriage that would be *legal* and one that would *not* be *illegal* (in the sense of exposing the individual to prosecution for bigamy) was clearly one that many people found difficult to grasp, given the frequent replies on this point in the advice columns of newspapers. Particularly in the late nineteenth century, there was both considerable uncertainty and a need for reassurance regarding any future remarriage. While some of the published responses merely noted that the questioner would not be guilty of bigamy if they remarried having heard nothing from their spouse for seven years, others emphasized that the second marriage would nevertheless be void if the first spouse later turned out to be alive. The *Sheffield & Rotherham Independent* did not pull its punches when it advised in 1891 that in this eventuality 'the second [marriage] will be illegal and void, the children born of it will be bastards, and her so-called husband will he at liberty to turn her out of his house and refuse to maintain her.'

Only from 1889 onwards was a genuine belief in the death of the first spouse accepted as a defence to the crime of bigamy regardless of whether the seven years had elapsed (see p. 104). Before this point, it was entirely possible that a marriage within seven years of a spouse's reputed death could be originally presumed to be valid by one court (for example when deciding on an individual's settlement for the purposes of the Poor Law) but held to be bigamous by another when it transpired that the spouse was in fact alive. After 1889, if the evidence was sufficient to convince a civil court that the first spouse had died, it is highly likely that a criminal court would also take the view that the remarrying spouse had done so in good faith, and acquit him or her of bigamy.

Q: *I've found an entry in a marriage register in 1836 describing the bride as 'supposed to be a widow, her former husband having been transported for life and the vessel lost in which he sailed.' Would it have been valid or was she risking prosecution for bigamy and transportation herself?*

A: If the woman in question had indeed received this news of her husband's supposed death, and had heard nothing further from him, the law would presume her second marriage to be valid in the case of any dispute. If the husband turned up alive and well within the seven-year period, however, the second marriage would be void and the wife liable to be punished for bigamy—although it is unlikely that she would be transported for the offence, as this was almost never ordered for female bigamists.

Q: *I've found an entry in a marriage register in 1837 describing the bride as widowed 'by transportation of first husband'. The first husband had been sentenced to transportation over seven years earlier. Would the wife really have been regarded as a widow in such a case?*

A: As we have seen (p. 117), there was a common but mistaken assumption that the transportation of one spouse entitled the other to remarry. The *Morning Post* noted humorously in 1806 that: 'When a man is sent to Botany Bay for bigamy, it is called a *transporting* divorce.' But while this might have been a common understanding of the situation, the phrase was certainly not a legal one: transportation did not act as any kind of divorce. Before 1828, an absence overseas for seven years would act as a defence to bigamy, but would not end a marriage; after that date it would in addition be necessary to show that the left-behind spouse had not heard anything from or of the departed spouse during that time.

Q: *I remember that in Hardy's* Far from the Madding Crowd *Bathsheba promises that she will marry Boldwood once seven years have passed since the supposed drowning of her husband Troy. Would she really have needed to wait this long?*

A: At the time of the publication of the novel in 1874, such a delay would certainly have been advisable, despite what seems to be clear evidence of Troy's death (his abandoned clothes having been found on the beach and an eye-witness account of him being carried away by the current). The law is portrayed as demanding a wait of seven years; religion as requiring that she at least *believe* her husband to be dead; while the ardent (but self-interested) Boldwood argues that 'every reasonable person' thinks she could marry straightaway. In the event, of course, Troy turns up just after the promise has been given and is shot and killed by the maddened Boldwood—leaving Bathsheba truly a widow and free to marry the faithful Gabriel Oak.

Decrees of presumption of death and dissolution of marriage

The seven-year period was also the basis of a further piece of legislation passed in 1937. This allowed an individual to obtain a 'decree of presumption of death and dissolution of marriage' if they had not heard of their spouse for the previous seven years; such a decree ended the first marriage even if the absent spouse was still alive, and allowed the other to contract a valid marriage. If the absent spouse did later turn up alive, he or she was simply faced with a *fait accompli*—their first marriage had ended.

THE EXPECTED DURATION OF MARRIAGES

It is commonly claimed that in past centuries most marriages lasted for little more than ten years, with individuals dying in early middle age. But as family historians will know from perusing burial records, estimates of life-expectancy—calculated as they are from the average life-span from birth to death—are seriously skewed by high rates of infant mortality. Throughout the seventeenth and eighteenth centuries, around a fifth of newborns died before their first birthday, and as late as 1901 it was still the case that a fifth died before the age of ten. Those who managed to survive the dangerous years of early childhood could look forward to a considerably longer life-span: life expectancy at the age of 5, 10, 20, or 30 was very different from that at birth. In fact, a man who had reached the age of 30 in the first decade of the nineteenth century could expect to live for a further 30 years; a century later, he could expect to live to the age of 70.[†]

So, while life expectancy at birth tended to hover between 30 and 40 years for much of the period covered by this book, only edging

† Houlbrooke, p. 2

above 50 in the twentieth century, the proportion attaining older ages was by no means negligible. Even in the seventeenth and eighteenth centuries there were those who survived into their 80s or older. Demographers have estimated that 9% of the population was over the age of 60 in the seventeenth century, and 10% in the eighteenth; while it fell back slightly, to only 7% in the nineteenth, this was on account of the increasing number of young people in the population rather than a decreasing number of the old. To put this in numerical terms, in the 1821 census there were over 434,000 individuals over the age of 60, including 124 centenarians, while by 1891 the census recorded 1,376,390 individuals over the age of 65.

Of course, the duration of a marriage depends upon the longevity of *both* partners. Epidemics might suddenly wipe out a whole section of the community, healthy and sickly alike, and bring a marriage to an unexpectedly sudden end. While plague virtually disappeared after the 1660s, epidemics of smallpox, typhus, cholera, and influenza still wreaked occasional havoc on the population.[†] But, perhaps surprisingly to us today, survival rates did not vary greatly by gender. While women had to face the potential perils of childbirth, these have perhaps been exaggerated. One demographic study examining the risk of dying in or as a result of childbirth has estimated that in the late seventeenth century there were 11.6 maternal deaths for every 1,000 births, but that by the first half of the nineteenth century this had more than halved to 5.5.[‡] In the intervening years the rate had fallen fairly steadily, with the exception of the second half of the seventeenth century when it rose to 15.7 deaths per thousand births, reflecting the general rise in mortality in this period and the greater vulnerability to other infectious diseases of women who had just given birth. If anything, wives were more likely to outlive their husbands than *vice versa*, for the simple reasons that they tended to be younger than their husbands as well as having a slight edge in terms of life-expectancy.

So how long did marriages in past centuries actually last? We can get some indication from studies of past communities. A study of widows in Abingdon in the early seventeenth century, for example,

[†] Houlbrooke, p. 3
[‡] Schofield

found that their marriages had on average lasted around 18-20 years.[†] The case study of Cardington indicates that those residing in this Bedfordshire parish in the late eighteenth century had marriages lasting an average of 28 years (see further p. 173). Examples can be found among the inhabitants of both very short and very long marriages: Richard Brown's first marriage to Margaret Pell had lasted less than a year before her death; by contrast, Joshua and Elizabeth Crockford had married in 1757, when both were in their early twenties, and clocked up 65 years of married life before dying a few months apart in 1823.

Moving into the nineteenth century, the marriages of those resident in the Northamptonshire village of Kilsby in 1851 lasted on average for 36 years, with those bereaved having usually attained the age of 60 before experiencing the death of a spouse. Again, some of the marriages were long by any standards: Samuel Bailey and his wife

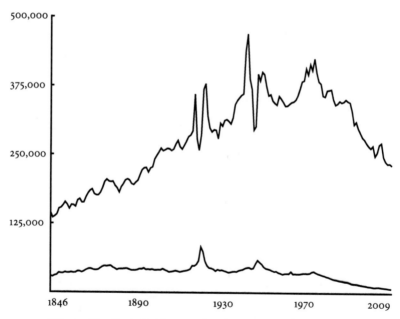

Fig. 4.1 *Number of widows and widowers remarrying (bottom) compared to total marriages (top), 1846-2009*

† Todd

Mary, both in their 70s at the time of the 1851 census, had married in 1800 and were to be together for another 13 years before Samuel's death in 1864 at the age of 91. Interestingly, the marriages of those living in the rather insalubrious district of Neithrop in Banbury had also lasted for an average of 36 years.

For more recent generations the statistical information available allows us to construct a typical life-course. A woman born in 1860 could expect to marry around the age of 26 and to lose her husband at the age of 59 before dying herself at the age of 64: a total of 33 years of marriage and 5 years of widowhood. A generation on, and the average age at marriage had dropped slightly and longevity increased, resulting in an estimated 38 years of marriage and 5 years of widowhood. This trend continued, with the result that a woman born in 1921 could expect to marry at 24, and have 44 years of married life and 6 years as a widow.[†] So, most of the married population did not experience the loss of a spouse until relatively late in life. Of course, a problem with such averages is that they may conceal a considerable range of experiences. Since our focus in this chapter is on remarriage, we will now turn to considering the factors that might influence whether or not a bereaved spouse would remarry.

THE CHANCES OF REMARRYING

It may be helpful to start with some broad trends before drilling down into the detail. For the years before civil registration we are of course dependent on parish-level studies, whether singly or in accumulation, but certain trends are discernible. Basically, there has been a fall in the proportion of widows and widowers who have remarried over the past four centuries. It has been estimated that, while in the mid-sixteenth century around 30% remarried, this fell to a little over 10% in the mid-nineteenth century. Other studies suggest that the trend was generally downwards during the intervening centuries, although the precise level at any given time and place would depend on a whole range of factors: a sudden epidemic might strike down a significant proportion of the population, leaving individuals suddenly bereaved at a young age and increasing the proportion of remar-

† Gibson p. 117

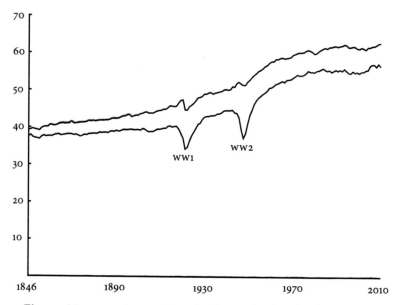

Fig. 4.2 *Mean age at remarriage of widowers (top) and widows (bottom), 1846-2010*

riages; low remarriage rates, on the other hand, might either indicate the longevity of first marriages or the lack of suitable partners for remarriage within small communities.

Age (Fig. 4.2)

By far the most important factor determining whether an individual remarried was the age at which they suffered the loss of their spouse. Of course, bereavement and remarriage might happen at any age. At one end of the scale there were those who experienced the death of one spouse and remarriage to a second before attaining the age of majority; this situation, though relatively rare, was contemplated by those responsible for drafting the Clandestine Marriages Act of 1753, which stated that parental consent would not be needed in the case of the second marriage. Occasional cases can be found in the registers: in 1886, for example, Harriett Brown, a 20-year-old widow, married a bachelor of the same age at St Botolph-without-Bishopsgate. Widowers, however, were much less likely to remarry while still minors, reflecting the fact that men tended to be a little older than women when entering into a first marriage. There were, conversely, remarriages at considerably older ages: the diarist Parson James Woodforde commented on a marriage in 1764 that took place in Somerset between 'an old farmer widower of 80 and a widow of 70', while the oldest widower recorded as remarrying at St Botolph-without-Bishopsgate in the period 1850-1921 had attained the grand old age of 84.

Despite such occasional examples of remarriage in old age, broadly speaking (and in line with what we might expect) the younger a man or woman was at the time of bereavement, the more likely they were to remarry. While it can be difficult to ascertain the ages of all individuals within a particular cohort, some work has been done on how the duration of a first marriage influenced the likelihood of a second. The study of remarriage in Abingdon in the first half of the seventeenth century (above, p. 156) found that widows who had been married for less than ten years were around three times as likely to remarry as those who had been married for more than twenty years; in the second half of the century this gap widened, with younger widows being even more likely to remarry and older ones even less so. Similarly, the Cardington case study (p. 173) shows that those who had remarried had markedly shorter first marriages than the norm, their average duration being under 14 years as opposed to over 28.

From the 1840s we have official data on the ages of all those who described themselves as 'widow' or 'widower' on their marriage certificate. While we know from other studies that individuals were not necessarily telling the truth about either their age or their marital status, the large size of the sample does mean that we can be reasonably confident in the accuracy of the overall estimates. The trends are clear: over the course of the nineteenth and twentieth centuries, the average age of widowers who remarried rose from just 40 in the 1840s to over 60, and the average age of remarrying widows from the late 30s to the mid 50s.

This steady increase in the age at remarriage reflects increased longevity and the decreasing likelihood of losing a spouse at an early age (with the exception of two sudden falls in the age of widows who remarried in the wake of the two world wars).

Gender

Men and women who lost a spouse at an early age, then, would usually expect to remarry. We see such expectations at work in Anne Brontë's *The Tenant of Wildfell Hall*: at the start of the novel, Helen Graham, who is passing as a widow, is advised by well-meaning neighbours that 'though you are alone now, you will not be always so; you have been married, and probably—I might say almost certainly—will be again.' Helen, it should be noted, is also described as 'excessively pretty' and only in her mid-20s!

Once past a certain age, however, women were much less likely to remarry than were men. This meant that the overall rates of remarriage for widowers were considerably higher than those for widows. Quite simply, different social expectations applied to the remarriage of men and women.

Throughout the seventeenth and eighteenth centuries, the 'virtuous' widow was expected to be chaste and loyal to the memory of her deceased husband, while the remarrying widow was thought to be displaying an unseemly desire for sex.[†] Contemporary literature warned that widows would be sexually demanding and prone to compare their new husband's prowess with that of their former love. As one saying had it, 'He that woos a maid, must fain lie and flatter, But he that woos a widow, must down with his breeches and at her.' The 1709 work *English Proverbs with Moral Reflexions* expanded upon this common sentiment:

> When a young jaunty Widow appears with so much borrow'd Lustre in her joyful Mourning, as Pride, Art, and Money can furnish, she might as well have hung out the sign of a second Marriage, with a tempting Motto upon it, of her first Husband's being quite forgotten in a Month's Time; or have put up a Bill at the Door, to tell the World, that this House is to be let, enquire within, and know farther, to your Satisfaction; for good Wine needs no Bush. Such a gay flaunt'ring Appearance of our faithless Relict will be as good as a *Noverint Universi* [i.e., 'let it be known'], that the Widow is a Woman still every inch of her, and a Wanton into the Bargain.

† Collins

The diarist Lady Sarah Cowper, writing around this time, clearly agreed with such views: noting the marriage of one woman past the age of child-bearing, she condemned her motivation as 'beastly'.[†] Such disapproving attitudes to widows' remarriage persisted even into the twentieth century. One woman interviewed towards the end of the century recalled that her grandmother 'used to say that once your husband had gone, you shouldn't look attractive to other men, that's why so many dressed in black'.[‡]

The motivations of the men who married widows were also seen as suspect, since they were often portrayed as marrying for reasons other than love. Again, Lady Sarah Cowper attributed the husband's motivation for the above-mentioned marriage to a desire for his new wife's money: 'Covetousness is thought to be his excuse (if it be one) for 'tis said she is rich.' And *Gnomologia*, an anthology of proverbs published in 1732, included the observation that 'A good season for courtship is when the widow returns from the funeral'.

The difficulties that this characterisation posed for widows were reflected by the diarist Katherine Austen, who provides us with a rare insight into the thoughts of a widow contemplating remarriage. Writing in the 1660s, Katherine disdained the idea of marrying for wealth, noting that 'a person... whose soul and heart may be fit for me is the chief riches to be valued.' Yet at the same time she was aware of the ridicule that a marriage for love alone might bring about, adding that there was 'a reflection of disrepute when women's inclinations are steered all by love.' Later, when courted by a physician, she prayed earnestly that she might be defended against temptation. She clearly felt that any second marriage would dishonour the memory of her dead husband, noting that her body could 'be enjoyed but by one'. Instead, she felt her suitor should be satisfied with 'those lawful intimacies of friendship and correspondences... which is the better part of me'.[1]

A widow, however long she lived after the death of her husband, might still be described as the 'relict' of her husband. There was no equivalent term to describe widowers, who were expected and even

† Quoted by Kugler, p. 72
‡ Sutton, p. 306
1 Todd (1997)

encouraged to remarry. As one historian of the Victorian era has noted:

> Young and middle-aged widowers were positively encouraged to return to work, and later to seek solace in a second marriage.... Dying wives and their friends frequently encouraged husbands to remarry in the interests of motherless children, as well as the assumed male need of 'sympathy and support'.[†]

Memorials erected to late wives were more likely to exhort their bereaved husbands not to grieve for them than were those erected to late husbands. There are a number of examples in the moorland church of St Mary's, Goathland, to this effect. One, memorialising a wife who died in 1825 aged 41, directed: 'Go home my husband and my child so dear/ And do not weep that I am sleeping here....' Another similarly encouraged her dear husband and children not to pine for her loss. Of course, we cannot know whether these epitaphs reflected the true wishes of the dying wife, since it would after all have been the husband who erected the memorial! But the more significant point is that such epitaphs, while not directly encouraging remarriage, did at least signal that there was tacit social approval for a bereaved husband to 'move on' at a later date. An important point to bear in mind here is that if widowers with young children did *not* remarry, it might be difficult for them to keep the household together: 'the death of a wife and mother often precipitated the breakdown of domestic economy and splintering of the family unit'.[‡] Children might be sent to live with relatives or neighbours, while those who were capable of earning a living might move out.

In any given community, then, there were likely to be considerably more widows than widowers: first, because more wives outlived their husbands than *vice versa* and, secondly, because those men who did outlive their wives were more likely to remarry.

Status and wealth

Alongside age and gender, the status and wealth of the bereaved spouse might also affect the likelihood of remarriage. Here, however,

† Jalland, pp. 176-77
‡ Strange, p. 200

the trends are much less clear cut, since the needs and wishes of the bereaved were often not matched by the opportunities available to them. In other words, a wealthy widow or widower would be a more eligible spouse than a poor one; at the same time, though, the poor might well have a much greater need to remarry so as to secure the services and support of a spouse.

For some women, the death of a husband at least had the advantage of conferring financial independence, and wealthy widows who enjoyed economic independence might be reluctant to risk entering into a second marriage. At the highest levels of society it was the usual practice for an agreement to be made on marriage specifying what provision the wife would receive in the event of the husband dying before her. While landed estates tended to be subject to arrangements to ensure that they passed to the eldest son or male heir, the widow of a wealthy man might well have the right to reside in a specific house, and such 'dower houses' still scatter the landscape. Men whose wealth took the form of cash rather than land—and so had greater freedom to leave their property as they wished—would often leave substantial amounts to their wives. Even if they did not, under the intestacy rules that applied in the absence of a will, a widow was entitled to half of her husband's personal property if there were no children, and a third if there were. As one 1732 book of proverbs recorded: 'The rich widow cries with one eye, and laughs with the other'.

Wealthy widowers were similarly cushioned from at least some of the impact of bereavement: for those able to employ a number of servants, the domestic role of the wife was less vital and could be replaced by a housekeeper, with governesses taking care of the children. An examination of patterns of remarriage in the Hertford-shire parish of Aldenham in the seventeenth and eighteenth centuries also found that widowers with property were significantly less likely to remarry speedily than those who had no property.[†]

Further down the social scale, however, the importance of a wife in running a household might make the need to remarry all the more urgent. One historian, examining remarriage in the north-east of England at the turn of the seventeenth century, outlines the various practical reasons for speedy remarriage:

† Griffith

On the death of his wife, a young yeoman or husbandman sought a replacement as soon as possible; without a woman's domestic labour there was no one to rear the children, tend the kitchen garden, the bees, cow or poultry, cook, spin or brew. Wives could be, and sometimes were replaced by servants (and older widowers could turn to a daughter or daughter-in-law) but for the young, remarriage was preferable, and for the childless, it was essential.[†]

Of course, many men would have had little or nothing to leave, and their widows would need to take on paid work, or otherwise be dependent on kin, charity, or local poor relief—the death of a husband has rightly been described as 'an economic catastrophe' for most households.[‡]

Studies of a number of villages in the second half of the nineteenth century show that the majority of widows, even those aged over 55, were in some form of paid employment, and that the proportion of widows undertaking paid work was considerably higher than for wives.[1] In London, meanwhile, the social investigator Charles Booth found widows pursuing 'diverse but overwhelmingly poorly paid occupations', including hawker, brush-maker, kite-maker, watercress-seller, coster, washerwoman and mangler, odd-jobber, charwoman, ironer, factory employee, matchbox-maker, and prostitute. While remarriage might well have been an attractive option for such women, it was not necessarily a readily available one: impoverished widows, particularly those with dependent children, were not a particularly attractive matrimonial prospect. Those unable to make ends meet would be obliged to seek assistance from the poor law. As the *Liverpool Review* put it in 1890:

> The poor struggling self-respecting widow can hold out no longer. The parish—that fated and hated name!—must be appealed to, and thus the terrible descent is made from the happy, self-supporting home down through weakening efforts and narrowing opportunities to the parish and the grave.

At the same time, the widespread recognition of the difficulties faced by widows meant that support from the parish was made available

† Chaytor
‡ Laurence, p.64
1 Rose

on more generous terms than was the case for widowers. In addition, charitable provision also tended to be more generous for widows than for widowers. Almshouses were very often founded upon the Biblical precept that there was a particular obligation to care for widows. The Morley College almshouses in Winchester, for example, bear a stone plaque reminding onlookers of St Paul's words to Timothy: 'Now she that is a widow indeede and desolate trusteth in God and continueth in supplications and prayers night and day'. Bishop Cosin's almshouses in Durham were founded in 1666 to provide accommodation for four men and four women, who were given a room and an annual stipend of £6/13/4d. in quarterly instalments, but only so long as they remained unmarried. On a more worldly level, legend has it that Roger Pemberton's almshouses in St Albans were founded to atone for his accidentally killing a poor widow with a bow and arrow. When it came to financial help, the majority of charitable legacies directed that funds be provided simply for 'the poor', with local trustees left to decide who was most deserving. In the church at Turvey, Bedfordshire, for example, is a wall-board recording some fourteen bequests, of which half are for the benefit of 'poor' or 'necessitous' parishioners; two of these bequests specify widows, but none specify widowers. In the Hertfordshire parish of Royston, 26 shillings was left to 'poor widows and widowers', but such specific mention of widowers is very much in the minority.

Some widows, then, would have felt that a guaranteed, if modest, sum from these sources was preferable to the unpredictability of a second marriage. As one historian has pithily pointed out, 'marriage to a poor man entailed more poverty, not security'.

Key Fact: The availability of charitable funds and poor relief meant that it could make more economic sense for a bereaved woman to remain a widow rather than remarry.

The role of emotion

It is important, though, not to overlook the importance of more intimate and subjective factors in the discussion of broader trends and statistics. The fact that in past centuries the untimely loss of a family member was a common experience has led some to infer that our ancestors must have had a less emotional attitude toward death and bereavement than we do today, and that remarriage would be a purely practical matter for a bereaved spouse. One very eminent historian even argued that, at least before the eighteenth century, 'evidence of close affection between husband and wife is both ambiguous and rare'.[†] More recent historians have, thankfully, profoundly disagreed with this idea, drawing attention in particular to the affection expressed in wills, on memorials, and in the grief-stricken responses of the bereaved to the death of a spouse. One nineteenth-century miner, recording the death of his wife, commented that 'my very soul seemed to lose hope somehow, and sent me adrift on a dark and trackless future—lonely and desolate without her. We had braved the storm and ruthless tempest in all its fury for 40 years'.[‡]

The consensus today would seem to be that there is: 'little evidence that individuals guarded against the possibility of "premature" bereavement by limiting their emotional involvement with members of their families; much to show that they commonly suffered deep grief in the face of loss'.[1] The grief experienced on the death of a spouse (and, in addition, wider public attitudes toward how grief ought to be expressed) would obviously influence whether, and when, the surviving spouse remarried. While the feelings and emotions of our ancestors cannot be reconstructed from the bare facts of parish registers and census data, we can draw on the experiences of those who left diaries or autobiographies to try to imagine what they might have been.

THE NATURE OF SECOND MARRIAGES

When did people remarry?

A criticism commonly levelled at the bereaved—in particular widows—was that they remarried too quickly. The author John Dunton, for example, writing in the late 1600s, commented somewhat bitterly that:

> We in these days do not weep and mourn at the departure of the dead so much nor so long as in Christian duty we ought. For

[†] Stone (1977), p.88
[‡] Quoted by Vincent, p. 241
[1] Houlbrooke, p. 23

husbands can bury their wives and wives their husbands with a few counterfeit tears... contracting second marriages before they have worn out their mourning garments.

Despite the fact that criticism focused on remarrying widows, it was in fact widowers who were more likely to remarry within a short period of being bereaved. One detailed demographic study of remarriage in the seventeenth and eighteenth centuries found that the median interval between bereavement and remarriage was just over a year for men (12.6 months) and around seven months more for women (19.4 months).[†] Within this period, the findings from a number of other studies suggest that rapid remarriage was more common for both men and women in the seventeenth century than in the eighteenth, and also more common in the first half of the century than the second. Class also played a role: poorer men were more much likely to remarry speedily than the better-off. As one historian has suggested, a very rapid remarriage might well have been 'the result of desperation rather than choice'. Particularly where the wife had died as a result of giving birth, a widower might be left with a young infant to care for.

Whom did the bereaved remarry? (Figs. 4.3 and 4.4)

It is possible to observe within the remarriage patterns of bereaved spouses certain broad trends that stand out from marriage patterns between spinsters and bachelors. Widowers who remarried were more likely to marry a spinster than a widow; widows, by contrast, were just as likely to marry a widower as a bachelor.

This can be seen in a sample of 17,422 marriages in St Botolph-without-Bishopsgate between 1754 and 1921: 10% involved widowers marrying spinsters, 6.3% widows marrying bachelors, and 6% widowers marrying widows.

These patterns played out against a range of advice literature that counselled widows against marrying a bachelor younger than herself. In *The Whole Duty of a Woman* (1797), a writer named William Kenrick sternly warned widows:

† Schofield and Wrigley

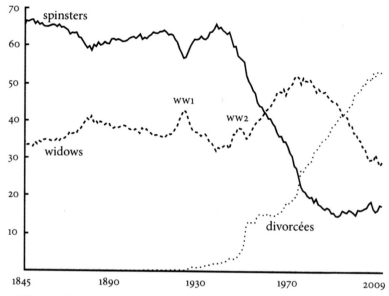

Fig. 4.3 *Remarriages of widowers (%) by brides' marital status, 1845-2009*

Art thou antient, yet seekest the embraces of a young spouse, he will be the bane of thy latter days; he will bring jealousy to thine heart and misery to thy gray hairs. He will think himself a living body tied to a dead carcase, and hold thee loathed in his sight.

Equally, men could be warned against the risks of marrying women much older than themselves, with all the problems of mismatched affection this might bring: in a 1746 tract entitled *The Folly, Sin, & Danger of Marrying Widows & Old Women in General, Demonstrated; & Earnestly Address'd to the Batchelors of Great Britain by a True Penitent*, a clearly embittered man who had called off his engagement to a young woman worth £200 in favour of the 65-year-old widow of an apothecary, worth some £5,000 but of a very ill temper, wrote: 'I have myself been married to an Old Woman, and what is worse, a Widow; but, I thank God, my Wife died a few Weeks ago.'

From 1845 until the mid-twentieth century

The Registrar-General first began in 1845 to publish national-level statistics on who was marrying whom, and from this point through

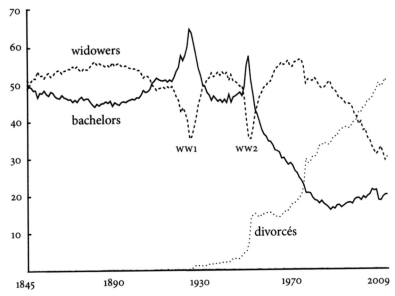

Fig. 4.4 *Remarriages of widows (%) by grooms' marital status, 1845-2009*

to the end of the Second World War we can observe certain very consistent trends in remarriage among the bereaved, and particularly among widowers. Throughout the remainder of the nineteenth century and up to the First World War, just under two-thirds of remarrying widowers married spinsters, with the remaining third marrying widows. The precise proportion varied a little year by year, but never fell below 59% or rose above 67%. The figure dipped a little during the war, but recovered during the 1920s and 1930s. The 1940s saw the figure falling again, and 1949 was the last year in which half or more of all remarrying widowers married a spinster.

By contrast, from 1845 to 1900 just over half of remarrying widows married widowers rather than bachelors. The first decade of the twentieth century saw remarriages to bachelors becoming slightly more common, and this trend accelerated during the First World War and its aftermath, with such marriages accounting for almost two-thirds in 1919, as the number of young widows soared. After that, however, there was a swift reversal to the nineteenth-century

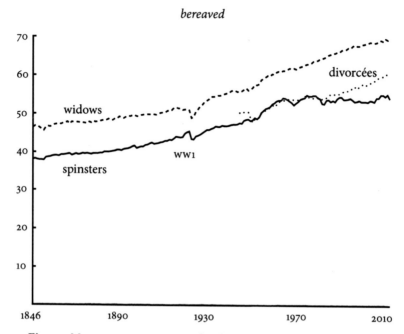

Fig. 4.5 *Mean age at remarriage of widowers by brides' marital status, 1846-2010*

pattern of slightly over half of widows remarrying widowers, and this remained the position until the Second World War.

> **Key Fact: Before the late 1940s, the majority of remarrying widows married a widower, while the majority of remarrying widowers married a spinster.**

The most significant change in the wake of the Second World War was the growing popularity of a third option—that of a widow or widower remarrying someone who had been divorced. Such remarriages had been taking place throughout the period, but in such small numbers as to be statistically invisible before 1920. In that year, just 1% of remarrying widows and widowers married a divorcee. In the wake of the Second World War this jumped into double figures: whereas in 1942 only 3% of widows had married a divorced man, by 1946 this had risen to 7% and within the year it had doubled to 14%. The increase was only marginally less dramatic for widowers.

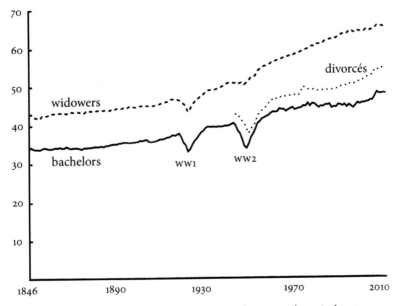

Fig. 4.6 *Mean age at remarriage of widows by grooms' marital status, 1846-2010*

From the mid-twentieth century

From the 1950s onward, though, the patterns look very different: remarriages between widowers and spinsters dwindled, both in absolute and proportionate terms, as did remarriages between widows and bachelors. Between the mid-1950s and the early 1990s, widowers were most likely to marry widows, and vice versa. In the 1990s, however, remarriages to a divorcee became the most common option for both widows and widowers, and by 2010 such marriages were in the majority. Such trends illustrate how modern marriage patterns differ from those of past generations.

Age at remarriage (Figs. 4.5 and 4.6)

There were equally clear patterns in the average age of the remarrying spouse according to whether their new spouse was single, bereaved, or divorced. Throughout the period for which official records exist (from 1845 onwards), the average age at remarriage of a widower marrying a spinster has been noticeably lower than the average age of a widower marrying a widow. Information on the age of those marrying a divorcee only became available in the 1940s, when the average was close to that for those marrying spinsters; since then, however, it has increased at a faster rate.

Similar patterns can be seen for remarrying widows, although the effect of the two world wars on age at remarriage is much more marked: unsurprisingly, the average age of remarrying widows dropped markedly during and after both conflicts.

Spinsters and bachelors who tied the knot with widowers and widows tended to be older than those whose spouse had never previously been married. From the 1840s to the 1940s, bachelors marrying widows tended to be around ten years older than those who married spinsters, and the same was true for spinsters marrying widowers. The gap widened still further during the second half of the twentieth century, to around 15 years, reflecting the increase in the average age at remarriage after bereavement. From these rather dry statistics, we can infer something of our ancestors' attitudes toward remarriage—it seems that the same expectations applied to remarriages as to first marriages: husbands were, on average, a little older than their wives, but too great a disparity might be looked at askance.

CASE STUDIES OF REMARRIAGE PATTERNS

Two case studies of specific communities will help to put these broad statistical trends into context:

(i) Cardington in 1782

The Bedfordshire parish of Cardington was the subject of an early census, drawn up by an enterprising local in 1782. The level of detail available makes it a wonderful source for historians, especially as there is nothing to indicate that Cardington residents were special in any way other than fortuitously having their details recorded; and other work that has been done on Cardington also means that we have insights into the lives of its parishioners beyond the bare census. When we look at first marriages, for example, we can see that Cardington men and women (with average ages at marriage of 26 and 24 respectively) were pretty much in line with contemporary trends:

most only ever married once, with the average duration of marriages being 28 years but some lasting for considerably longer.

In 54% of cases, it was the husband's death that ended the marriage. Widowers were, however, around *twice* as likely to remarry as were widows: 67% of those who remarried after bereavement were men. And in general, those who remarried had had considerably shorter marriages than those who did not remarry: where the surviving spouse entered into a second marriage, the average duration of the first marriage had been only 13.8 years, whereas the average duration of the marriages of those who did not remarry was more than twice this, at 29 years.

Most people who remarried did so within a relatively short time, the average period between bereavement and remarriage being 3.4 years. Of course, an average may conceal dramatic differences: one individual married after only four months, while another waited 13 years!

Only a very few Cardington parishioners married for a third time, but examples of such complex matrimonial histories nonetheless help to illuminate the range of possibilities. Elizabeth Ashwell, for example, was a widow in her mid-thirties at the time of the census in 1782. Her first marriage, in 1772, had been to a much older man, himself a widower, whose own first marriage had taken place way back in 1744. Elizabeth went on to marry a second widower in 1783, and a third husband in 1788. Thomas Braybrooks, meanwhile, had already clocked up three marriages by the age of 40: his first had lasted just over 12 years, but his second—to a widow—only 10 months. Each time, he remarried relatively swiftly, contracting his second marriage within six months, and his third within a year and a half.

(ii) Kilsby in 1851

The marriages of couples living in the Northamptonshire village of Kilsby at the time of the 1851 census lasted for an average of 36 years. With the average age at bereavement being in the early 60s, remarriage was correspondingly rare. Even among those bereaved at this late age, however, remarriage was not unknown.

Two of the women who experienced the loss of a husband before the age of 40 remarried. Ann Capell was 33 when her husband died in 1863, and she remarried the following year. Her new husband, William Crock, was also from Kilsby; ten years older than her, he too had lost his wife the previous year. The 1871 census saw them living together in Kilsby with a child from each former marriage and a four-year-old son of their own. Amelia Flanders was even younger, just 29, when her first husband died at the age of 30 in 1852. She was not native to Kilsby, and may well have returned to her home parish of Irchester after her husband died, as her second marriage took place close by and the 1861 census found her living there with her new husband. Theirs was a blended step-family, with six children from his first marriage and three children from hers. Somewhat surprisingly, on the date of the next census they were living separately—she with *his* children in Pavenham, and he with *hers* in Irchester!

By contrast, none of the women who were over the age of 40 at their husband's death remarried. Sarah Bennett lost her husband in her early 40s, when she had four children aged 12 or younger; she remained a widow for 40 years before her death in 1902. Louisa Gunthorpe, widowed and childless at the age of 41, went to live with relations in Bradford after the death of her husband in 1861; she too was to have a long widowhood of almost 40 years.

For men, remarriage followed a slightly different pattern, in that the cut-off point was 50 rather than 40. The only man to experience the loss of a spouse before the age of 40 was Joseph Prestage; his wife died when he was in his mid-30s, and he remarried within a matter of months. The speed with which he remarried was unsurprising, given that he had several young children at the time of his wife's death; in addition, his family had moved to London, and he was unlikely to have relatives close by to provide support and assistance.

In addition, *all* of the men (six) who were bereaved in their 40s remarried. The three who did so most quickly all had children, and all married widows. William Marsh, a nail merchant in his mid-40s, married Mary Hicks a few months after the death of his wife; the subsequent census saw them resident in Kilsby with children from each of their former marriages. Thomas Bayes, a baker, was 40 with two children when his wife died, and he remarried just over a year after her death. The third widower was William Crock, whose remarriage to Ann Capell was described above; Ann was the only one of these three remarrying widows to be *younger* than her new husband, and also the only one who went on to bear children in her second marriage.

But the presence of children did not automatically lead to a swift remarriage: Samuel Frisby was just 40 when his wife died, leaving him with three children, the youngest of whom was aged just 5; Samuel, however, waited eight years before remarrying a 35-year-old spinster in 1860. Whether he did so for companionship because his children were no longer living with him, or whether his second marriage precipitated their departure from the family home, we do not know, but certainly neither of his surviving children were living with him and their stepmother at the time of the 1861 census.

Nor was it only widowers with children who remarried relatively swiftly. John Leatherland's first (and much older) wife died in 1853, and he remarried in November of the following year—to Samuel Frisby's younger sister Elizabeth, then in her late 30s.

The final widower to be bereaved in his 40s was Thomas M. Stubbs, a tea merchant. He was almost 50 when his wife died, and he had no children to look after (or be looked after by); at the time of the 1871 census, four years after his wife's death, he was living in lodgings, but later that year he married a 41-year-old widow with four children.

By contrast, *none* of the five men who were bereaved in their 50s remarried, although there was one widower—Joshua Crock—who remarried at the age of 65, within two years of losing his first spouse and after 42 years of marriage.

CONSTRAINTS ON REMARRIAGE

Financial

We have already seen that a widow of independent means might be reluctant to remarry and thereby give up control over her property to her new husband, at least before the Married Women's Property Act of 1882 gave wives control over the property they had brought to the marriage or inherited. But another risk was that remarriage would itself lead to the forfeiture of any property she had inherited from her late husband—if, for example, he had included a 'condition' in his will that it would pass to their children if she remarried.

The law on conditions in wills is incredibly complex (and for the most part, you might be pleased to learn, unnecessary for our purposes!). In its simplest terms, the courts were willing to ignore clauses that tried to prevent individuals from marrying at all. So, if a testator left somebody a sum of money in their will but stated that the recipient would forfeit the money if they married, a court would simply disregard that condition; the intended recipient would inherit the money whether or not they married. But a different approach was taken in relation to *re*marriage. In the late eighteenth century, the then Lord Chancellor, Lord Thurlow, ruled that 'a condition that a widow shall not marry is not unlawful.' In other words, such a condition would be upheld, and a widow who remarried in defiance of it would forfeit the promised inheritance. Of course, there was a limit to what could be recovered of any lump sum if it had already been spent by the time the recipient remarried. In practice, therefore, inheritances to which such conditions were attached more often took the form of an annuity (which would simply stop being paid upon remarriage) or land (which the recipient could only continue to occupy so long as they did not remarry).

While most of the cases involved restrictions that testators had placed on the remarriage of widows, in the 1875 case of *Allen v Jackson* it was held that exactly the same rule applied to the remarriage of widowers. As Lord Justice James noted in that case, it had been 'considered to be very right and proper that a man should prevent his widow from marrying again', on the basis that a second alliance might threaten the interests of the children; this being the rationale, it would be 'monstrous' if a woman who left her husband property to care for their family could not also be able to stipulate that he would forfeit that property if he remarried.

Of course, even if the law said that a husband was entitled to include a condition limiting provision for his wife to the period of her widowhood, this by itself does not tell us whether husbands actually *did* so. It needs to be borne in mind that only a minority of husbands made wills at all, and it seems that only a minority of those who made a will included any restriction on their widow's remarriage. Those who did were not necessarily trying to control a former spouse's life; instead, they were more interested in protecting their children's rights against a future step-father. Such men might state that their widow would have to give a financial guarantee to ensure that the legacies destined for the children were protected if she remarried.

If a will included a condition that a widow would forfeit some or all of the property she had received from her husband if ever she remarried, what was likely to be its effect? Here it is worth bearing in mind that the reason we know about the reported cases is because the widow in question did remarry, and because those who would become entitled to the property brought the case to court. There were at least some widows who valued a second marriage above the continued enjoyment of property, but there may well have been others who did *not* remarry precisely because of a condition of this kind. We know that some widows tried to conceal a remarriage so that they could continue to receive financial benefits. One woman who remarried in her maiden name received short shift when she tried to argue that she was still entitled to the property bequeathed to her: the court declared that her remarriage was perfectly valid, and that as a result she had forfeited the property.

Legal

Restrictions as to timing

While a too-hasty remarriage after the death of a spouse might evoke social disapproval, there were no legal restrictions as to its timing; remarriage could in theory take place as soon as the first spouse had shuffled off this mortal coil and the necessary formalities (licence, banns etc.) had been observed. Indeed, the famous line in Hamlet's first soliloquy, 'Frailty, thy name is woman!' is bewailing the fact that his mother Gertrude had remarried less than a month after his father's death. He continues: 'A little month, or ere those shoes were old with which she follow'd my poor father's body, like Niobe, all tears... within a month, ere yet the salt of most unrighteous tears had left the flushing in her galled eyes, she married.'

Restrictions on marriage within the prohibited degrees

There was, however, an important set of restrictions on remarriage. For the majority of the period covered by this book the law took the view that marriage made husband and wife 'one flesh', and this mystical link survived the death of either of them, insofar as a relationship of affinity was still deemed to exist between the bereaved spouse and their late spouse's relatives. As a result, prohibitions existed regarding marriage with former in-laws, and so a widower or widow could be barred from marrying a deceased spouse's parent, child, grandparent, grandchild, sibling (full or half), uncle, aunt, niece, or nephew.

For a brief period under the Commonwealth (from June 24th, 1650, through to 1660) the restriction was narrowed to the former spouse of one's parents or child, or one's former spouse's parent or child. At the Restoration the old rules were restored, but the reduced power of the church courts led to a change in the consequences of such marriages: from the late seventeenth century, a marriage within the prohibited degrees could not be challenged after the death of either party. This meant that a marriage within the prohibited degrees between 1660 and 1835 was therefore *voidable* rather than void.

In 1835, however, there was a sudden and stark change of policy. Legislation which came into force on September 1st of that year provided that all marriages within the prohibited degrees were to be void rather than voidable, whether the couple were related by blood or by marriage. Existing marriages between in-laws, however, were to be regarded as valid, unless they had already been declared null, or were in the process of being challenged before the courts when the legislation was passed. Existing marriages between blood relations remained voidable.

So everything hinged on when exactly a couple had married. A marriage within the prohibited degrees entered into on August 31st, 1835, would have been voidable at that point, but validated the day after by the 1835 Act. Had the marriage taken place on September 1st, it would have been void from the start. The difference was a stark one: even a voidable marriage would be treated as valid unless it was actually annulled by a court. By contrast, a marriage that was void had no legal existence at all: neither party would have any rights against the other, and any children born to them would be illegitimate.

Marriage to a deceased wife's sister

But what did these prohibitions on marrying one's in-laws actually mean in practice? While the 1835 Act had clarified the status of marriages within the prohibited degrees, it had attracted considerable opposition. A little over a decade later, a Royal Commission reporting on the topic drew attention to the fact that the new legislation had not been conspicuously successful in preventing prohibited marriages. An inquiry into five sample areas revealed that no fewer than 1,364 marriages within the prohibited degrees had been contracted since the 1835 Act came into force, and that nine-tenths of these were between a widower and his deceased wife's sister. Some had initially been refused permission to marry by the authorities, but had managed to go through the ceremony elsewhere. Only 88 prohibited marriages were known to have been prevented by the 1835 Act, and in 32 of these cases the outcome was clearly thought to be even worse than a void marriage—'open cohabitation, without the sanction of any form or ceremony.' Based on these figures, and working on the assumption that the five districts surveyed covered only one-tenth of the population as a whole, one MP came up with the rough-and-ready (but nonetheless illuminating) calculation that there had been about 13,000 prohibited marriages in the previous eleven years, and that if each couple had had three children there would be 'nearly 40,000 children, whose claims to legitimacy could not be legally admitted.' While these figures obviously need to be treated with some caution and read in the light of the more than 1.5 million marriages that had taken place over the same period, they might still be thought to be surprisingly high.

Analysing exactly who entered into such marriages, the Commissioners noted that those marrying their former in-laws were not the usual type of outlaws; rather, many were 'persons of station and property, and of unimpeachable character and religious habits.' While such marriages were not common amongst the Victorian elite (who were less dependent on relatives for care and support and more vulnerable to public scrutiny), they were a frequent occurrence among the middle classes. Amongst the poorest, meanwhile, it was felt to be inevitable that a sexual relationship would develop between a man and his deceased wife's sister if she came to care for her nieces and nephews, on account of the lack of both space and privacy in poorer homes: some would go through an invalid ceremony, but others would live together without even the pretence of a marriage.

Those giving evidence to the Commissioners were also asked for their views on the morality or otherwise of marriage to one's deceased wife's sister and other former in-laws. One clergyman gave his view that such marriages were 'generally contracted from the most proper feelings, and in very many cases principally from an attachment to the former wife, either to her memory, or to the family from which she came.' Evidence was given of such marriages having the sanction of friends and family. The Chief Rabbi indicated that in Jewish law such marriages were regarded as 'laudable', and a dissenting minister similarly expressed his view—and that of his brethren—that such marriages should not be prohibited.

As a result of such evidence, the Royal Commission recommended in 1848 that the law should be changed. Nonetheless, despite almost annual attempts at reform, it was not until the first decade of the twentieth century that the prohibitions began one by one to be dismantled. The first to be lifted was that on marrying one's deceased wife's sister. The unimaginatively named Deceased Wife's Sister's Marriage Act of 1907 not only allowed such marriages to take place, but also validated those that had already been entered into. As a result, the effect was just as drastic as that of the 1835 Act: a marriage entered into on August 27th, 1907, would have been void on that date, yet retrospectively validated the day after; a marriage entered into on August 28th, 1907, would have been valid from the start. In the meantime, though, what actually happened to those who had entered into a prohibited marriage?

Q: *I've read that individuals could face criminal prosecution for entering into a prohibited marriage—is this true?*

A: No. This illustrates the confusion that the term 'illegal' generates. A marriage between a man and his deceased wife's sister was only 'illegal' in the sense of not being permitted by law; it was not a criminal offence. While in earlier centuries couples who married in defiance of the canon law might face proceedings in the ecclesiastical courts, by the nineteenth century this was rare.

The fact that their marriage was void meant that either party could simply decide to repudiate the other, and there is no shortage of examples of men and women simply upping and leaving. Since the law provided no redress in such cases, we tend only to learn about them if they came before the attention of a court for other reasons—as, for example, in the bigamy trial of James Chadwick, in 1846:

> James, then a labourer, had married his first wife Hannah in
> Manchester Cathedral in 1825. At the time of the 1841 census they
> had four children, ranging in age from 13 to just one year. Four
> years later Hannah died in childbirth, and a few months later James
> went through a ceremony of marriage with her sister Ann, again
> at Manchester Cathedral. They gave the same address, 9 Mount
> Street, which is where James had been living with Hannah: while
> addresses in marriage registers need to be treated with caution, in
> this particular case it seems likely that Ann moved in to look after
> the family in the wake of Hannah's death. The union lasted only a
> short while, however: James learned that it was illegal and went
> through a third ceremony of marriage with a woman named Eliza
> Bostock, this time at the church of St John. Before long, however,
> he found himself in the dock for bigamy, the prosecution having
> being brought by a group of men who had an interest in testing the
> validity of marriages with a deceased wife's sister. The verdict of the
> court was that his marriage to his deceased wife's sister was void
> and the marriage to Eliza was accordingly valid; he was, therefore,
> acquitted of any offence.

Obtaining documentary evidence of those deceased-wife's-sister unions that proved successful is perhaps even more difficult—happy marriages rarely leave a trace in the law reports—but we do have the account of one woman who wrote in to contribute to the debate over marriage in the pages of the *Daily Telegraph* in 1888:

> The seven years of our married life have been very happy ones (in
> our own and our large circle of friends' opinion we are as legally
> married in our Maker's sight as any princess of the blood); and to
> prove that in no way we repent our union, I can only assure you
> that had the Deceased Wife's Sister bill become law this session
> (as in common justice to thousands of women and children it
> ought to have done), and not been made retrospective, we should

have re-married, in order to make binding by English law the ceremony... which is still so absurdly deemed in this country alone illegal.

And we do know for certain that a number of these unions proved lasting, and that, from the evidence of wills and other arrangements made to take effect on death, some men felt a sense of obligation towards the women they had married. Of course, the only reason we know about these arrangements is because someone else had challenged them, but then the prospect of money might well cause relatives to turn on those who had previously been accepted as part of the family. While it was of course possible for either party to make a will that explicitly benefited the other, or their children, there was a clear sense that these 'marriages' could not be regarded as creating any legal rights or presumptions. As one judge rather damningly put it: 'I cannot consider this cohabitation, whether incestuous or not, as anything better than a state of fornication.'

Since marriage to a deceased wife's sister is an aspect of marriage law which has been raised by a great number of family historians with whom I have corresponded since the publication of *Marriage Law for Genealogists*, it is worthwhile answering some of the more common questions that have arisen:

Q: *I've found a marriage between my ancestor and his deceased wife's sister in a Register Office in 1898—would they have known it was invalid?*

A: This was a decade in which there were almost annual bills to change the law, and much public debate, so it would have been surprising if the couple had not known that their marriage was void. But they may well have felt, like many others, that such marriages *ought* to be legal. Marrying in the Register Office minimised the risk of any unsympathetic neighbours objecting, as since 1856 intended marriages had simply been announced by pasting up a notice outside the Office. Other than this, officials did not look into the couple's circumstances. In declaring that they were free to marry, the couple were however committing perjury.

Q: *I've found a marriage in 1893 between my ancestor and his deceased wife's daughter from a prior marriage—how would this have been seen at the time?*

A: Given how the debate focused so heavily on the case of the deceased wife's sister, it would not be surprising if some did not realise that other relatives of a deceased spouse also fell within the prohibited degrees. In one particular suit to annul a marriage of this kind, it was claimed that none of the parties, nor any of their friends and relations, had been aware of its invalidity at the time it was entered into. The husband did admit that he had learnt it was not valid within six months, but that he had only taken steps to have it declared void when his wife turned to drink.

Q: *I've found an ancestor who married his deceased wife's sister in December 1895—just a few months after the death of his wife—and who then married another woman in 1906. Was this last marriage legal?*

A: At the time he married his deceased wife's sister, the law was very clear that such unions were void. As a result, he was perfectly free to repudiate her without the need to seek a divorce or even a decree of nullity. Nor was she the only woman to have entered into a marriage with the widower of her deceased sister only to find herself abandoned for another woman later on. Others in that position tried to charge their supposed spouse with bigamy only to find that the new marriage was perfectly legal.

Q: *I've found an ancestor who married his deceased wife's sister, Lucy, in 1900 and died the following year leaving a legacy to 'my wife, Lucy'. Would she have been entitled to the legacy even though she was not legally his wife?*

A: Yes. The courts had to grapple with a number of similar cases where men left assets to a 'wife' who was in law no wife at all. In such cases judges tended to take the view that this was not a problem as long as it was clear who was meant by the word 'wife'.

Q: *What would have happened to my ancestor who repudiated his marriage with his deceased wife's sister and married another woman in 1906? Would the latter marriage have been invalidated as a result of the 1907 Act?*

A: No. Although the 1907 Act retrospectively validated all existing marriages of this kind, if either party to these once-prohibited marriages had lawfully remarried before the Act was passed, then the first marriage would remain null and void. By contrast, had the third marriage taken place just a year later—in December 1907 rather than December 1906—the outcome would have been very different: his marriage to his deceased wife's sister would by then have been retrospectively validated by the 1907 Act and his subsequent marriage would have been both void and bigamous.

Marriage to a deceased husband's brother

It was to be another fourteen years before the Deceased Brother's Widows Marriage Act 1921 was passed, which allowed a widow to validly marry her late husband's brother. Just as had been the case with subsisting marriages to a deceased wife's sister, so long as both parties were still alive and had not validly married somebody else in the meantime, then the marriage was retrospectively rendered fully valid from July 28th, 1921, onward.

Q: *I've found a marriage between my great-grandmother and her deceased husband's brother in 1899. They are described as 'married' in the 1901 census but as a 'widow' and 'unmarried' in the 1911 census, although by then they had several children. Why would they have changed the way they described themselves?*

A: At the time it was entered into, the marriage would have been void, and their children would therefore have been illegitimate. It is plausible that they did not realise this at the time, since it was the prohibition on a marriage to a deceased wife's sister that was the one more usually discussed. Perhaps the publicity given to the change in the law in 1907 made them realise that their marriage was not valid—which may explain the changes in the way they described themselves in the 1911 census. If they were both alive and still together in 1921, however, their marriage would have been validated retrospectively.

Ten years later, on July 31st, 1931, the bar on marrying a deceased spouse's aunt, uncle, niece, or nephew was similarly removed. For ease of reference, the following table summarises the status of different relationships at different times:

	Celebrated before September 1st 1835	Celebrated from September 1st 1835 onward	Valid from
Deceased wife's sister			Aug 28th, 1907
Deceased husband's brother	Voidable	Void	July 28th, 1921
Deceased spouse's niece, nephew, aunt, uncle			July 31st, 1931
Deceased spouse's child or parent			1986/2007

Table 4.1 *The changing legal status over time of certain marriages within the prohibited degrees.*

So even entering into a new marriage following a bereavement was not necessarily a simple matter, even if it was the statistically most common form of remarriage up until the Second World War. In the final chapter, by contrast, we shall turn to what was the *least* common form of remarriage—that where the same two people went through more than one ceremony together.

REMARRIAGE TO THE SAME PERSON

PLANNED REMARRIAGE
REMEDIAL REMARRIAGE
TACTICAL REMARRIAGE
PERSONAL MOTIVATIONS
WHAT WAS THE STATUS OF THE SECOND CEREMONY?

One intriguing discovery for any genealogist to make is that an ancestor went through more than one ceremony, but with the *same* person. There are perhaps a surprising number of cases where couples have gone through a second ceremony of marriage with each other—sometimes on the same day as the first, sometimes within a few weeks or months, and sometimes after the lapse of years or even decades. The motivations for such repeat marriages were extremely varied, but here I have grouped them into the *planned* (where it was clearly envisaged from the start that there would be two ceremonies), the *remedial* (where there was a concern that the first marriage might be invalid for some reason, or indeed a certainty that it wasn't valid), the *tactical* (where the first marriage was perfectly valid but there were external reasons for going through a second ceremony) and the *personal* (where for example the parties were celebrating an anniversary or going through a second ceremony for the sake of relatives who could not attend the first).

Before looking at these different categories, it is worth considering whether there was in actual fact a second marriage. On occasion, misunderstandings and mistranscriptions can lead to a single marriage being recorded with two different dates—what one might term a 'false' double marriage. This can often be a problem in the centuries before January 1st finally supplanted March 25th as the start of the legal year: prior to 1753, it should be borne in mind that marriages that took place between January 1st and March 24th were often (but not invariably) recorded as belonging to the *previous* year by today's reckoning. Finding two dates precisely one year apart for what otherwise appears to be the same marriage is a sign that this might be the reason. An apparent double marriage of the same bride and groom where the two dates are twelve days apart might indicate that a single event has been recorded under both the Old Style (Julian) calendar and the New Style (Gregorian) calendar. Obtaining the original marriage certificates or checking the physical register to look at the entry in its date context should resolve such cases. Similarly, some sources may give the impression that the date the banns were read was the date of the marriage; again, checking the original will clarify what the actual date was and whether there were indeed two ceremonies.

Another trap—but one that is more difficult to detect—is where there is a 'concealed' double marriage. This is where the fact that the two ceremonies involved the same parties is disguised by the fact that they used different names on different occasions. In the case of Henry Cecil, whom we met earlier (p. 80), his second marriage to Sarah Hoggins appears to be his first, since at the time of the actual first marriage he was passing by the name of 'John Jones'. In that particular case, of course, Henry had a very good reason for assuming a false name, being already married at the time, but there are other cases in the records where the reason is more obscure—as in the 1858 marriage of Thomas Hewitt who married in the name of James Baker. His bride, on discovering the truth, insisted on being married a second time with him using his real name.

Of course, in some cases we may never be able to identify the reason why a particular couple went through more than one ceremony of marriage. Where an ancestor went through *three* ceremonies in swift succession—as in the case of William Slark and Anna Maria Hancock, who married at St Luke in December 1818, at St Botolph in May 1819, and at St Pancras in August 1819—one begins to suspect that some parishes were offering some kind of dole or benefit to poorer members of the community upon marriage, but this must remain speculation unless the relevant minute books, accounts, or papers of the parishes concerned have survived and contain clues; nor should we rule out the possibility that some couples remarried purely on a romantic whim. But at least by looking in detail at some of the known reasons for remarrying we can start to whittle down the possibilities....

PLANNED REMARRIAGE

We will start with the situation where the two marriage ceremonies are so close in time that both must have been planned together. The most obvious explanation is that one set of rites would not have been recognised by the law but nonetheless had religious or emotional significance for the couple. More difficult to interpret are those cases where both ceremonies were potentially ones that the law would recognise, but some possible explanations can nonetheless be offered.

Legal recognition and religious conscience

There were always a number of couples who would, then as now, plan to go through two marriage ceremonies: one that was in accordance with their religious beliefs, and one that satisfied the law's requirements. Such double ceremonies were usually close together, often on the same or consecutive days. In thinking about who might do this, why, and what form each ceremony might take, we will look briefly at the reactions to civil marriage under the Commonwealth and then at the position before and after the Marriage Act 1836.

Under the Commonwealth

In 1604, the Church had reiterated the need for all marriages to be preceded by either banns or licence and celebrated in the parties' home parish, though it did not go so far as invalidating marriages that ignored these requirements. The religious and political foment of the time led many to marry in a parish other than their own, but even more dramatic change occurred during the Commonwealth when, between 1653 and 1660, civil marriage replaced the Anglican ceremony. Since the civil registrars who recorded marriages during these years generally served a number of parishes, some parishes appear to have celebrated no marriages at all; the likelihood here is that they were recorded in another parish's register. You may well find that some ancestors married twice: as one sceptical bride noted in her diary, she would not have believed herself legally married had it 'not been done more solemnly afterwards by a minister.'

From 1660 to December 31st, 1836

Before 1837, the only recognised form of marriage was one according to the rites of the Church of England, but this affected different faiths and denominations in various ways (for more detail on this aspect of the law, see 'How your ancestors married' in *Marriage Law for Genealogists*). Jews were seen as being governed by their own religious law and were exempted from the 1753 and 1823 Marriage Acts, and it was only in 1836 that their marriages were brought within the framework of the law. Quakers had the benefit of the same extensions, although the status of their marriages was more disputed. Other Protestant non-conformists had not developed their own specific marriage rites and complied with the Anglican rites, if somewhat unwillingly. By contrast, ever since the Reformation there had always been Catholic gentry households where priests carried out the nuptial rites: for these individuals, a further Anglican ceremony was necessary if they were to be legally married. Catholic ancestors are, therefore, the most likely to have gone through a double ceremony.

Examples of such double ceremonies can be found across the country: at the Catholic stronghold of Coughton Court in Warwickshire, almost 100 Catholic marriages took place in the second half of the eighteenth century; for every one, a corresponding Anglican ceremony can also be traced. The favoured option was for the Catholic ceremony to take place on a Sunday, presumably when the couple attended Mass, with the Anglican ceremony held either the same day or the following day, largely depending on the distance that needed to be travelled between the two. In London, with its many churches, it was particularly easy for couples to go through both ceremonies on the same day. The parents of the architect Augustus Pugin, for example, went through such a double ceremony on February 2nd, 1802, marrying in the Anglican church of St Marylebone and also having a full Catholic rite and nuptial blessing at the French Catholic Chapel in Portman Square, a fifteen-minute walk away.[†]

† I am grateful to Sylvia Dibbs for this information.

Q: *I have found that my ancestors married in a Catholic chapel in the late eighteenth century. Where should I look for the Anglican ceremony, and when would it have taken place?*

A: The key thing to remember in searching for the Anglican marriage is that those marrying in the Church of England had a far wider range of places to choose from. Although the law stipulated that couples should marry in the parish where at least one of them was resident, the residency periods were relatively short and clergymen did not always check whether the couple had fulfilled them. Nor did marrying in a parish to which the parties did not belong invalidate the marriage. Those living in or close to large towns and cities might well choose to marry somewhere where they could be effectively anonymous, especially if they did not subscribe to the same religious tenets as their neighbours. That said, the distances travelled between the Catholic ceremony and the Anglican marriage were generally short. The case-study of Coughton Court, for example, shows that 70 of the 95 couples in question travelled three miles or less, while a further 19 travelled between three and nine miles, and only six couples travelled farther afield—anything up to 21 miles. In most cases, moreover, there was evidence that the parish in which the Anglican marriage took place was the one where they were resident.

Q: *I have found a record in a non-conformist chapel in 1800, stating that my ancestors were married there. Was their marriage invalid or should I be looking for an Anglican ceremony as well?*

A: The first thing to check in such a case is whether the chapel was actually conducting marriages. There are examples of chapels recording that members of their congregation had married, when the marriages in question actually took place elsewhere. If it is clear from the register that the ceremony of marriage was celebrated in the chapel, then it would certainly be worth looking for an Anglican ceremony as well—marriages in non-conformist chapels had no legal standing before 1837, and were consequently rare.

After January 1st, 1837

Two key changes were made by the Marriage Act 1836: it introduced the possibility of marrying according to civil rites or in a non-Anglican religious ceremony. One might then expect the need to go through a double ceremony of marriage to have disappeared. However, matters were not quite so simple. The 1836 Act did not give blanket legal effect to non-Anglican ceremonies, but rather to those conducted in a non-Anglican place of worship that had been registered for marriage. Since by no means all such places of worship were registered for marriage, there were still many couples who might feel the need for a legally recognised second ceremony. Indeed, it is even possible that the number of double ceremonies *increased* after 1837, as Protestant dissenters developed their own marriage services and an expectation of being able to marry according to their own rites. And, of course, they no longer had to go through an Anglican ceremony for legal validity, but could choose the civil option of marrying in a Register Office.

REMEDIAL REMARRIAGE

The 'remedial' category covers two main types of cases: those where the first marriage was initially assumed to be valid, with some potential flaw only later coming to light; and those where both may well have known that it was invalid but been unable to do anything about it at the time.

After discovery of a technical defect

If the second marriage followed swiftly upon the first and was celebrated in the same church, then a likely explanation is that the couple or their families had realised (or been told, perhaps by the minister who had conducted the ceremony) that there was some minor or technical problem with the first marriage and so took steps to remedy it as soon as possible. Such mistakes might be particularly likely to occur after the law had changed on a particular point, as this example from the Hampshire parish of Oakley in 1768 indicates:

> the first Publication of the banns between Thos. Small and Jenny
> Benham were made (thro' a mistaken conformity to the Rubrick

in the Common Prayer Book) on Easter-day, Easter Monday, and Easter Tuesday, and the first marriage was accordingly solemnized. But, upon perusing the Marriage Act of the 26th of George the 2nd, which orders the Banns to be published on Three Sundays, it was thought proper to publish the Banns afresh on the 1st and 2nd Sundays after Easter, and a Marriage between the above mentioned Parties was again solemnized after such fresh Publications.[†]

Similarly, when William Brown married Sarah Sargent in Bradford-on-Avon, the banns were by mistake called in the name of Sarah *Sartain*. The register records that the banns were republished in the correct name and the marriage resolemnised.

In these cases it was certainly possible that the parties would not have been validly married without such remedial action. In other cases, though, going through the second ceremony seems to have been overcautious. In 1858, the *Morning Chronicle* reported the case of a double marriage where the first had been solemnised by a German clergyman, but, the parties having 'some doubts as to its perfect legality', a second was then performed according to the rites of the Church of England, in a Protestant church at Cheltenham.

Some seemingly technical defects assume a different significance when later events are taken into account. There are a number of examples of men marrying women in false names, going through a second remedial ceremony of marriage when the deception was discovered, but then abandoning them altogether and going through a third, bigamous ceremony with another woman. In such cases one is forced to wonder whether the false name was assumed in the hope of later being able to deny the marriage:

Elizabeth Barker married the resplendently pseudonymous 'George Adolphus Fitzmaurice Mortimer' in 1858, but then discovered his real name was the less impressive one of James Peacock. While the marriage would have been perfectly legal despite this, one can understand why she insisted on being married a second time; another ceremony of marriage was accordingly gone through. He subsequently deserted her and went through a further ceremony

[†] Quoted in Fearon and Williams, p. 27

of marriage with another woman, this time adopting the name
of Richard Mortimer Peacock. Elizabeth succeeded in obtaining a
divorce on the basis of his adultery, bigamy, desertion, and cruelty.

After death or divorce

But what if the first ceremony between the parties had been void on account of one of them being already validly married? Sometimes one or both would have been aware of this impediment, while in other cases they might have genuinely believed that they were free to remarry. The circumstances in which individuals might enter into void marriages of this kind have already been examined in the chapter on bigamy (pp. 101 ff); for now, our interest lies with those cases where the couple took remedial action and remarried when they were finally free to do so.

> *Caroline Pantland Hughes married Joseph Thomas Morant in 1853,*
> *when both were in their teens. After he enlisted in 1859 and was sent*
> *out to India, she returned to her parents and in 1864 went through*
> *a ceremony of marriage with John Thorne. When Joseph returned*
> *in 1872, he gave her into custody for bigamy. Technically she had no*
> *defence but was nonetheless acquitted. Moreover, Joseph received*
> *short shrift from the Old Bailey when he asked whether he was*
> *to have his wife back, the Commissioner describing his request as*
> *'preposterous' on account of the fact that he had not communicated*
> *with her for 13 years. John, meanwhile, had loyally told the court*
> *that 'a good wife she has been to me', and Caroline returned to live*
> *with him after the trial. Their relationship clearly had its ups and*
> *downs: in 1874 Caroline charged John with assaulting her and told*
> *the court that since the trial his temper had become so crabbed that*
> *she no longer wanted to live with him. At her request he was bound*
> *over to keep the peace, despite his protestations that he loved her*
> *and would not harm a hair of her head. Whatever the truth of this*
> *incident, there was clearly a subsequent reconciliation. Joseph died*
> *in the first quarter of 1876 and within a few months Caroline and*
> *John had married. Still together at the time of the 1911 census, they*
> *recorded the duration of their marriage as being 44 years, clearly*
> *calculating it from the date of their second, legal, marriage.*[†]

† *Proceedings of the Old Bailey*, August 19, 1872; *Daily News*, August 12, 1874

If you have found two marriages of the same people many years apart, then, it is worth checking and rechecking whether either was previously married to a spouse who had died in the interim.

Rather rarer, but not unknown, were cases where a couple divorced and then remarried each other. The *Morning Post* reported on such a case occurring in Birmingham in 1864, while 10 years later the litigation generated by the matrimonial entanglements of George Henry Wildes illuminated the factors that might lead to a remarriage to one's own ex-spouse:

> *In March 1867, George Henry Wildes married Evelyn Charlotte Gladstone at St James, Westminster. Four years later he petitioned for divorce on the basis of her adultery and the decree was made absolute on August 5th, 1873. Within a week of this he had proposed marriage to a Miss Nuttall, a young lady of both 'great personal and mental attractions' and considerable wealth. Arrangements were duly made for their marriage to take place within the next three months. Matters then took a surprising turn. A few days before the wedding was due to take place, his first wife sought an interview with him and her explanation of her conduct led to a reconciliation between them. George wrote to his fiancée to convey his regret at having to break off the match but excusing himself on the basis that he would be committing a 'great sin' if he went ahead with the marriage in the light of the new evidence. Instead, he remarried Evelyn in the local Register Office; intriguingly, she chose to pass by her married name on this occasion. It was observed by one newspaper that this was only the second instance in which divorced parties had married each other since the establishment of the Divorce Court. The jilted Miss Nuttall, however, did not see this as a cause for celebration and successfully sued George for breach of promise of marriage, receiving £3,000 by way of damages.*

Sadly, such remarriages were not always any more successful than the original marriage. In 1870, the *Birmingham Post* noted the still more unusual case of a remarriage that was followed by a *second* divorce! In this case the parties had married in 1862 and divorced in 1866 on the basis of the husband's adultery and cruelty; a year later the illness of their child had led to a reconciliation and a remarriage, but the second marriage proved to be even shorter than the first.

TACTICAL REMARRIAGE

The 'tactical' category covers those cases in which there was some external pressure or incentive to go through a second ceremony—whether from the authorities, family, or friends.

'Enforced' Anglican ceremonies

Although the 1836 Act had explicitly stated that a non-Anglican marriage according to the methods set out would have exactly the same status as one celebrated in the Church of England, not all Anglican clergy shared this view. Some clergymen insisted that marriage was a sacred rite that should still be celebrated according to the ceremonies of the Church of England, regardless of the range of options now available, and persuaded their dissenting parishioners to go through a second ceremony. The incumbent of Frome in Somerset attracted attention in the national press when he persuaded a couple who had been married in a Wesleyan chapel to be remarried in church in 1854, and an indignant letter was sent to the Home Office complaining that it was 'reprehensible' that clergymen 'should be so bigoted as to conceive it right thus to disturb the minds of Parties so married, inducing them to ponder whether they have not been living in fornication and whether their issue be illegitimate.' A pragmatic solution was adopted, with legislation in 1856 providing for the possibility of a blessing in the Church of England following a marriage according to other rites.

Elopements and family weddings

Where a couple had eloped in order to marry without the knowledge of their parents, they might well go through a second ceremony to which family and friends could be invited, even if there was no doubt as to the validity of the first marriage. Sometimes the fact of the marriage may have persuaded their respective families of the pair's love for each other and the second ceremony would be a genuine celebration with loved ones. In other cases the family may have only grudgingly accepted the first marriage and have insisted that the couple go through a second ceremony so that there could be no gossip in the wider community about the status of the couple.

The most notorious destination for eloping couples was, of course, Gretna Green, and it seems that it was quite common for informal (and often hasty) Scottish weddings such as these to be followed by a ceremony on the English side of the border. This was perhaps overcautious—the English courts had refused to annul a Gretna Green marriage in 1769, which was taken as evidence of its legality—but the desire for legal certainty reflects the rather dissolute reputation that such ceremonies had acquired.

Two contrasting stories show couples going through an English ceremony of marriage after getting married at Gretna—but with very different outcomes:

Benjamin Howes and Mary Ann Kerney married for the first time in April 1822, at Gretna Green. Six weeks later they went through a second ceremony of marriage at St Leonard's Church, Shoreditch, having had the banns called there. So far this is no different from the many couples who went through a second ceremony of marriage in England after having married at Gretna, but then the pair went through a third ceremony of marriage four years later at St Dunstan in the West! The clue to this third marriage may lie in the combination of two facts. First, the banns had been called in the name of Mary Ann, whereas the bride had been christened with the single name of Mary. Secondly, shortly after their wedding in 1822 the London Consistory Court had annulled a marriage on the basis that the banns had been called in the wrong name—as with Mary, a middle name had been added for no apparent reason. While this was an uncharacteristically strict decision (judges normally looked at whether the additional name had disguised a person's identity), the court case would have given Benjamin and Mary a reason to go through another ceremony, just to make sure of the validity of their marriage.†

In 1838, William Amos Wilson, a veterinary surgeon from Liverpool, proposed marriage to Mary Simpson, and they ran off to Gretna to be married. In 1846, 'to make the marriage surer', they went through a second ceremony of marriage at St. Martin's Church in Liverpool. Unfortunately, in this case there had been a more serious

† I am grateful to Patrick Cunningham for sharing the details of this with me.

impediment to the validity of the first ceremony than simply the location: Mary Simpson had previously been married at Gretna to one Richard Carruthers, a butcher from Carlisle, who was still alive at the time of both the subsequent ceremonies. When William learned the truth of Mary's prior marriage is unclear, but it was not until 1858, when he wanted to remarry someone else, that he prosecuted her for bigamy. Despite the validity of her first marriage, the court refused to convict her, sympathising with the fact that it had taken place when she was only 16 as something of a frolic. Nonetheless, the upshot was that William was a bachelor and free to remarry just as he had wished.

Marrying 'on the strength'

If the groom was serving in the army then another reason for a second marriage presents itself: soldiers needed permission from their commanding officer in order to marry. Such permission would only be granted after a certain length of service and was dependent on the good conduct of both soldier and sweetheart. Emma Borrington, for example, who married Joseph Fearncombe in 1854, explained that 'he applied to his commanding officer for leave [i.e., permission]; my character from my place had to be sent up, and then leave was given.'

In addition, only a certain number of soldiers in each regiment were permitted to be married at any one time. The limit was set at about 6% of the regiment's strength in most cases.[†] A wife recognised by the army could lodge with her husband in the barracks and could earn money by cooking and washing for the regiment. Some were even permitted to accompany the regiment when it was posted overseas, although the rules here were even more restrictive, and wives would draw lots to determine whether they could go. Without permission to marry, a soldier's wife was simply not recognised by the army at all.

The consequences of not having permission can be illustrated by the case of Thomas Spencer, who married Ann Lilley in 1839. Since he had not been given the permission of his commanding officer to marry, he was obliged to separate from her the very day after the wedding. Within a week she had clearly decided that this was no basis

† Venning, p. 15

for married life, and apart from a few letters there was no communication between them. Many years later, she went through a second ceremony of marriage with another man, and in 1851 found herself charged with bigamy.

A wife denied the right to live with her soldier husband might reasonably have thought that the lack of permission invalidated the first marriage; similarly, a husband told that he needed such permission might feel he was free to repudiate a marriage entered into without such permission, as a number of other bigamy trials attest. In 1855, for example, Joseph Fearncombe stood trial for bigamy but explained that his first marriage had taken place while he was a deserter from the 4th Regiment, and that even his wife had not considered it a valid marriage and had often threatened to leave him. In fact, the permission of one's commanding officer was only necessary for the purposes of the army, and marriage without it was nevertheless valid. A second ceremony between the same parties was simply to ensure that the soldier had a marriage certificate that post-dated the grant of permission and so allowed his wife to follow the regiment.

So if you have a soldier ancestor who went through two marriage ceremonies to the same person that were some time apart, you can infer that a place 'on the strength' had become available between the two ceremonies. A number of examples that have appeared in family history magazines over the past few years indicate that the gap between the first and second marriage might range from a few months to a number of years.[†] Even if the marriage certificate does not identify the groom as a soldier, you might be able to find evidence of his occupation from census returns, for example if he is resident in army barracks. If his wife is there too, this would confirm that he had had permission to marry.

---

† See e.g. *Family Tree Magazine*, February 2013, p. 78 (Richard John Ashford married Annie Earls in Dublin in 1891, and again at Farnham Register Office in 1896); *Family Tree Magazine*, August 2013 (just over two months between the two marriages of John Abbott and Elizabeth Lett). I am grateful to Brian Pollard for these examples.

PERSONAL MOTIVATIONS

Sometimes, of course, the parties' families might not even know that there had been a prior marriage ceremony: the couple might have gone through with it as a declaration of their commitment to each other and then returned to their respective homes and families until such time as it became convenient to make their intentions public.

Q: *My ancestors married for the first time in 1860; both were stated as being of age but the bride was in fact only 19. Both continued to live with their respective families but exactly a year later they went through a second ceremony of marriage, this time in the presence of relatives. What would explain this, and is it relevant that both marriages were celebrated 'after Superintendent-Registrar's Certificate'?*

A: This sounds like a classic case of a couple marrying without the knowledge and consent of their families. They would have had good reason to marry by Superintendent-Registrar's Certificate in both cases, although this was—and continues to be—rare, since the vast majority of Anglican marriages were solemnised after the calling of banns. The Certificate was intended to be the civil equivalent of banns—it *had* to be used for non-Anglican marriages, but could also be used for Anglican ones. Up until 1856, a couple's intention to marry was read out at meetings of the Poor Law guardians—after that date, the notice of the intended marriage was posted up in the Register Office. So it had a degree of publicity—but in practice of course no one would find out about it unless somebody had reason to go to the Register Office. Using this option for the first marriage ensured that the families were unlikely to find out about it; using it for the second ensured a degree of privacy lest anyone object that they were already married!

One high-profile example of a double ceremony of this kind involved two of the Bright Young Things of the 1920s:

Daphne Winifred Louise Vivian and Henry Frederick Thynne, Viscount Weymouth, (later Marquis of Bath) had reason to marry secretly, as their relations objected to the match. They married by licence, in disguised names, and no friends or relations attended their marriage at St. Paul's Church, Knightsbridge, in 1926.

When their families later came round to the idea of them marrying, Daphne and Henry decided not to confess that they were already man and wife for fear that it would lead to trouble and distress. They became officially 'engaged', entered into various property settlements, and in 1927 went through a second wedding at St. Martin-in-the-Fields. This time around, the list of notable attendees took up several newspaper columns, the bride was followed by a train-bearer, four pages, and ten bridesmaids, and Princess Victoria sent her a ruby and diamond brooch.

No mention ever seems to have been made of the first marriage, and even when the pair subsequently divorced the date given to the court was that of the second ceremony. Only after both had remarried, and the wife had published her memoirs, did the truth come out, resulting in litigation all the way to the Court of Appeal to sort out the legal mess. It was finally decided that the divorce had dissolved the status of marriage, not a specific ceremony, otherwise their subsequent marriages would both have been void.

In other cases the family were aware of the first marriage but still wanted an opportunity to celebrate with the couple. In 1953, the *Daily Mail* reported the planned *third* wedding of a 23-year-old German girl to a staff-sergeant in the US airforce. Their first wedding, a civil ceremony, had taken place in Frankfurt in 1950; he was then posted to Prestwick and the couple went through a second ceremony in the church there. The third was to take place following his demobilisation in Lancaster, Pennsylvania, for the sake of his mother, who had been unable to attend the first two.

WHAT WAS THE STATUS OF THE SECOND CEREMONY?

The status of the second ceremony would depend on the status of the first. Where the first was merely a religious ceremony that had no legal status, or was flawed in some way and would have been regarded as void in the eyes of the law, then the second ceremony would be the legally effective one.

By contrast, if the first marriage was valid then the second ceremony was of no effect. In one early twentieth-century divorce case a judge was asked to dissolve both the first (valid but secret) marriage and the second (open but ineffective) ceremony but gave the suggestion short shrift, saying that the second could not be a marriage because they had already been married, that he could only dissolve actual marriages, and that if people 'chose to go through idle ceremonies he should not assist them'.

Since by definition the parties did not declare their true marital status in these cases, would they have been committing any offence in going through the second ceremony? At common law, it was a criminal offence to make a false oath. In 1801, John William Bishop, previously acquitted of bigamy, was convicted at the Old Bailey for swearing on oath that he was a bachelor. The judge emphasised 'the enormity of the offence' and sentenced him to two years in Newgate, plus a session in the pillory.

By contrast, the statutory penalties for inserting false details in the register originally applied only to the clergyman celebrating the marriage. Under legislation passed in 1823, an individual making a false oath was liable to forfeit any property that would otherwise come to them as a result of the marriage, but only where one or both was underage and marrying without parental consent. It was the Marriage Act 1836 that first introduced the possibility of an individual being guilty of perjury for 'knowingly and wilfully' making a false declaration for the purpose of bring about a marriage. In practice, though, this provision tended to be used against those who were going through a second ceremony of marriage with a different person, rather than someone to whom they were already married, and so you are unlikely to find any legal proceedings being taken against your ancestors for giving false details. The downside (for us!) of the law's reluctance to take action over such technical infractions is that the reasons why any particular couple went through more than one ceremony of marriage together will often have to remain a matter of speculation—but it is hoped that this chapter has given an idea of the most likely reason under different scenarios.

Get in Touch

For many of us, all we will know of our ancestors' marriages is the date of the marriage, its mode of celebration, and its duration. Understanding what happened during the marriage poses greater challenges in the absence of diaries, letters, or other documentary evidence. Unhappy marriages are, however, more likely to leave some kind of trace in legal records, and reports of court proceedings can often, as we have seen, be a rich source of information.

But what of those who escaped the notice of the law? It is very difficult to give any reliable estimate of the extent of informal separation and bigamy. Largely unevidenced claims that both must have been 'common' in an era of limited divorce do not get us very far. We know that both occurred, and on a scale to attract attention, but at the same time there is nothing to suggest that the proportion of couples splitting up was equivalent to that evident today. So marital breakdown in past centuries might have affected somewhere between 1% and 40% of marriages—an estimate too wide to be useful. But while novelists can claim omniscience over their created worlds, cautious academics and family historians should not theorise ahead of their data!

On the other hand, investigating the life histories of sufficient cohorts to be able to make confident claims about social trends of this kind would take several lifetimes. So this book is intended as part of a conversation. As noted in the preface, many of the questions addressed in its pages come from family historians; in return, I would like to put out a plea for information from those who have found bigamous, separated, divorced, or remarried ancestors to share their findings with me. For example, having built up databases of those prosecuted for bigamy, amassing data on those who remained undetected during their lifetimes would allow us to see whether there were differences between the two groups that explained why some escaped detection, and might give us clues about the overall extent of bigamy. Already I have had a number of family historians share the details of their ancestors' bigamous marriages with me, and in return I have been able to put their findings in context and even, on occasion, to tell them that their ancestor featured in an important legal case!

And those who are seeking further information are also very welcome to get in touch. So if you haven't found the answer to a particularly puzzling marriage in the preceding pages or in *Marriage Law for Genealogists*, please do contact me via the website and I will do my best to provide an answer:

warwick.ac.uk/dbb

BIBLIOGRAPHY

Anderson, O. 'State, Civil Society and Separation in Victorian Marriage' (1999) 163 *Past & Present* 161.

Annal, D. and Collins, A. *Birth, Marriage & Death Records: A Guide for Family Historians* (Pen & Sword, 2012).

Bailey, J. *Unquiet Lives: Marriage and Marriage Breakdown in England, 1660-1800* (CUP, 2003).

Chaytor, M. 'Household and Kinship: Ryton in the late 16th and early 17th centuries' (1980) 10 *History Workshop Journal* 25.

Collins, S. 'A Kind of Lawful Adultery: English Attitudes to the Remarriage of Widows, 1550-1800' in Jupp and Howarth (eds) *The Changing Face of Death: Historical Accounts of Death and Disposal* (Macmillan, 1997).

Cretney, S. *Family Law in the Twentieth Century: A History* (Oxford University Press, 2003).

Fearon, W.A. and Williams, J.F. (eds) *The Parish Registers and Parochial Documents in the Archdeaconry of Winchester* (Warren & Son, 1909).

Gibson, C.S. *Dissolving Wedlock* (Routledge, 1994).

Griffith, J.D. 'Economy, Family, and Remarriage: Theory of Remarriage and Application to Preindustrial England' (1980) 1 *Journal of Family Issues* 479.

Hammerton, A.J. *Cruelty and Companionship: Conflict in Nineteenth-Century Married Life* (Routledge, 1992).

Haskey, J. 'Marriage rites: Trends in marriages by manner of solemnization and denomination in England and Wales, 1841-2012' in Miles, Mody and Probert (eds) *Marriage Rites and Rights* (Hart, 2015).

Horstman, A. *Victorian divorce* (Croom Helm, 1985).

Houlbrooke, R. (ed) *Death, Ritual and Bereavement* (Routledge, 1989).

Jalland, P. 'Death, Grief and Mourning in the Upper-Class Family, 1860-1914' in Houlbrooke (ed) *Death, Ritual and Bereavement* (Routledge, 1989).

Kugler, A. '"I feel myself decay apace": Old age in the diary of Lady Sarah Cowper' in Botelho and Thane (eds) *Women and Ageing in British Society Since 1500* (Longman, 2001).

Laurence, A. 'Godly Grief: Individual Responses to Death in Seventeenth-Century England' in Houlbrooke (ed) *Death, Ritual and Bereavement* (Routledge, 1989).

McGregor, O.R. *Divorce in England: A Centenary Study* (Heinemann, 1957)

Menefee, S.P. *Wives for Sale: An Ethnographic Study of British Popular Divorce* (Blackwell, 1984).

Owen Williams, B. *Planning Your Wedding Day from A to Z* (W Foulsham & Co Ltd, 1964).

Parker, M. 'The Draft Nuptial Agreements Bill and the abolition of the common law rule: "swept away" or swept under the carpet?' (2015) *Child & Family Law Quarterly*.

Phillips, R. *Putting Asunder* (Cambridge University Press, 1988).

Probert, R. 'The Double Standard of Morality in the Divorce and Matrimonial Causes Act 1857' (1999) 28 *Anglo-American Law Review* 73; 'The controversy of equality and the Matrimonial Causes Act 1923' (1999) 11 *Child & Family Law Quarterly* 33; *Marriage Law and Practice in the Long Eighteenth Century: A Reassessment* (CUP, 2009); *A Noble Affair: the remarkable true story of the runaway wife, the bigamous earl, and the farmer's daughter* (Brandram, 2013) (with Shaffer, J. and Bailey, J.); (ed) *Catherine Exley's Diary: the life and times of an army wife in the Peninsular War* (Brandram, 2014).

Roberts, E. *Women and Families: An Oral History, 1940-1970* (Blackwell, 1995).

Rose, S.O. 'The varying household arrangements of the elderly in three English villages: Nottinghamshire 1851-1881' (1988) 3 *Continuity & Change* 101.

Rowntree, G. and Carrier, N. 'The resort to Divorce in England and Wales, 1858-1957' (1958) 11 *Population Studies* 188.

Savage, G. 'Intended Only for the Husband: Gender, Class, and the Provision for Divorce in England, 1858-1868' in Garrigan (ed) *Victorian Scandals: Representations of Gender and Class* (Ohio UP, 1992); 'The Instrument of an Animal Function: Marital Rape and Sexual Cruelty in the Divorce Court, 1858-1908' in Delap, Griffin and Wills, *The Politics of Domestic Authority in Britain since 1800* (Basingstoke: Palgrave Macmillan, 2009); 'They Would if They Could: Class, Gender, and Popular Representation of English Divorce Litigation, 1858-1908' (2011) 36(2) *Journal of Family History* 173.

Schofield, R. 'Did the Mothers Really Die? Three Centuries of Maternal Mortality in "the World We Have Lost"' in Bonfield, Smith, and Wrightson (eds) *The World We have Gained: Histories of Population and Social Structure* (Oxford University Press, 1986); (with Wrigley, E.A.) 'Remarriage Intervals and the Effect of Marriage Order on Fertility' in Dupâquier, J. *et al* (eds) *Marriage and Remarriage in Populations of the Past* (Academic Press, 1981).

Stone, L. *The Family, Sex and Marriage in England 1500-1800* (Weidenfeld & Nicholson, 1977); *Road to Divorce: A History of the Making and Breaking of Marriage in England* (OUP, 1990).

Strange, J-M. *Death, Grief and Poverty in Britain, 1870-1914* (Cambridge University Press, 2005).

Sutton, M. *We Didn't Know Owt: A Study of Sexuality, Superstition and Death in Women's Lives in Lincolnshire during the 1930s, 40s and 50s* (Shaun Tyas, 2012).

Todd, B. 'The remarrying widow: a stereotype reconsidered' in Mary Prior (ed) *Women in English Society 1500-1800* (Routledge, 1985); 'Demographic determinism and female agency: the remarrying widow reconsidered... again' (1994) 9 *Continuity & Change* 421; 'I do no injury by not loving: Katherine Austen, a Young Widow of London' in Valerie Frith (ed) *Women & History: Voices of Early Modern England* (Irwin Publishing, 1997).

Venning, A. *Following the Drum: The Lives of Army Wives and Daughters* (Headline, 2005)

Vincent, D. 'Love and Death and the Nineteenth-Century Working Class' (1980) 5 *Social History* 223.

Wright, D. 'Well-Behaved Women Don't Make History: Rethinking Family, Law, And History Through An Analysis Of The First Nine Years Of The English Divorce And Matrimonial Causes Court (1858-1866)' (2005) *Wisconsin Women's Law Journal* 211.

Index

Index

CPSIA information can be obtained
at www.ICGtesting.com
Printed in the USA
LVOW10s1213230717
542318LV00011B/385/P